WOMEN
IN SOCIETY

SOUTH AFRICA
DEE RISSIK

MARSHALL CAVENDISH
New York • London • Sydney

Reference edition published 1993 by
Marshall Cavendish Corporation
2415 Jerusalem Avenue
P.O. Box 587
North Bellmore
New York 11710

© Times Editions Pte Ltd 1993

Originated and designed by
Times Books International, an imprint of
Times Editions Pte Ltd

Printed in Singapore

Cover picture by Paul Weinberg/Southlight

Library of Congress Cataloging-in-Publication Data:
Rissik, Dee. 1953–
    Women in society. South Africa / Dee Rissik.
      p. cm. — (Women in society)
    Includes bibliographical references and index.
    Summary: Examines the experiences of women in South African society, discussing their participation in various fields and profiling the lives of significant women.
    ISBN 1–85435–504–X :
    1. Women—South Africa—Social conditions—Juvenile literature.
[1. Women—South Africa. 2. South Africa—Social conditions.] I. Title. II. Series: Women in society (New York, N.Y.)
HQ1800.5.R57 1992
305.42' 0968—dc20
                  92–12374
                  CIP
                  AC

Women in Society

Editorial Director	Shirley Hew
Managing Editor	Shova Loh
Editors	Goh Sui Noi
	Roseline Lum
	June Khoo Ai Lin
	Debra Fernando
	MaryLee Knowlton
	Junia Baker
	Sue Sismondo
Picture Editor	Nancy Yong
Production	Edmund Lam
Design	Tuck Loong
	Ong Su Ping
	Ang Siew Lian
Illustrations	Eric Siow/AC Graphic

Introduction

The women of South Africa come from a wide variety of cultures, races and creeds. They come from a population that is a mixture of many different African tribes, hosts of different European immigrants and a number of different cultures from Asia.

Unfortunately this diverse population does not as yet form a well-knit nation. The major cause of the rifts among the different groups in South Africa is the policy of apartheid, or separate development.

Under the apartheid system people were grouped into "Africans," "whites," "Coloreds" and "Asians." These groups were not supposed to intermix by marriage nor were they allowed to live in the same neighborhood. In every walk of life they were supposed to be segregated. There were separate schools, separate public transportation, even separate public toilets.

The government even felt it necessary to make a number of "homelands," rural areas, where people from the different African tribes were made to live. Only under exceptional circumstances were these people allowed to move to the urban areas to live and work. Those that already lived and worked in the cities and towns were forced to live in designated black neighborhoods—as were the Colored and Asian populations.

Such unnatural social conditions caused innumerable hardships and severe impoverishment, particularly to the majority of the women in the country. *Women in Society: South Africa* will look at the varying roles afforded to women both by their different cultural heritages and by the fragmented conditions imposed on them by government laws.

Due to internal as well as international pressures the government of South Africa has in recent years been forced to scrap the apartheid laws. The country is embarking on a path toward a just and democratic future, a future of equality for all people.

Contents

chapter one

African Rain Queen

Opposite: The regal African Rain Queen, Modjadji V, in her ceremonial leopard skin robe.

Right: The oldest seed-bearing plants in the world, cycads grow in great abundance close to the Modjadji royal residence. Often called the Modjadji Palm, the tall, majestic cycad has been protected by generations of rain queens.

The sound of the cowhide drums rolls down the verdant hillside and rumbles across the mist-shrouded valley, heralding a tribal ceremony, perhaps the rain-making rituals. Loyal subjects may get a glimpse of their queen, Modjadji ("mod-JA-ji") V, the African Rain Queen, dressed in ornate leopard skins and other ceremonial regalia as she sets about her mystical rites.

Legends tell us that perhaps the original princess fled from her father's kingdom in the Monomatopas and traveled southward. It is said she took the rain-making secrets with her.

She was with child, her brother's child. Rather than incur the drastic consequences of her kingly father's wrath, she and her loyal subjects left what is today called Zimbabwe, crossed the great Limpopo River, and set up her kingdom in the mountains that form the northern tip of the great southern African range, the Drakensberg. Her descendants still live in this eastern area of the Transvaal, a province of South Africa.

That first queen was the founder, over 400 years ago, of the present dynasty of Modjadjis who have since ruled the Balobedu tribe, a people whose past and present are shrouded in this enduring legend that blends romance with fact.

The rain-making secrets have been jealously and faithfully guarded by the Balobedu ever since. Only the queen knows these secrets, and she imparts them only to her chosen female successor.

The importance of rain

Understanding the importance of the legend of the African Rain Queen is easier when seen against the background of the importance of rain to South Africa. A large portion of the country's population has always been involved in agriculture despite the fact that the average rainfall is not very high, nor constant. This sometimes leads to droughts that cause enormous hardship, loss of cattle, and even loss of life.

For example, the average annual rainfall in the Johannesburg area in 1953 was about 25 inches, while in 1967 it was nearly double that at 46 inches. In the drought years of the early '80s, 1982 hit a low of 24 inches, while in 1988 it was again as high as 41 inches. The average rainfall in the Rain Queen's domain is over 30 inches a year, while an adjoining area just to the north averages only 16 inches a year.

Her successor

It is believed the reigning African Rain Queen, Modjadji V, although only middle aged, has already chosen her successor. By custom her choice is not made known, but it is widely thought to be her daughter—in keeping with tribal traditions.

As the Rain Queen is not supposed to marry, she takes women from the kraals of her headmen and they become her "wives." The biological fathers of these wives' children have no rights over them as the queen is considered their "father." Although the queen cannot marry, it is an unguarded secret that she chooses mates for herself from among the most prominent and powerful of her chiefs. Their daughters are in line as her descendants.

Some historians, discussing the female leadership of the Balobedu, have described as unique the fact that through the ages the tribe maintained good relations with neighboring tribes without having to go to war. Within the tribe they have upheld law and order without resorting to force.

Severe drought

It is also true that drought has rarely, if ever, affected the Rain Queen's domain. It is said the heavens never disappoint her loyal subjects or those who believe religiously in her powers to make rain.

Some have pointed out that her territory lies on the edge of a steep mountain range, and that the topography encourages the higher levels of rainfall responsible for the rich abundance of tropical foods such as mangoes, pawpaws or bananas, which grow in the shadow of Modjadji's palace. This deep valley, often enveloped in low-lying thick cloud, is still called Duiwelskloof, the Valley of the Devil, indicating the awe mixed with suspicion that many, in earlier times, held of this clan in which women hold the power.

Living legend

Modjadji V has immense social presence and poise and is ultimately responsible for maintaining the Balobedu tribe. Even the most senior of tribal elders closest to the queen are expected to address her on their knees as no one may stand taller than the queen.

Anybody approaching the *moshate* ("mo-SHA-tee"), the royal residence, must walk barefoot across the circular tribal court, the *kgoro* ("KHO-ro"), and must remain barefoot in the presence of the queen.

But at the same time Modjadji V cuts a very motherly figure, especially to her "wives'" children. She dresses simply for day-to-day life in the royal residence, a neat white thatched home surrounded by the dozens of thatched *rondavel* ("rond-A-vel"), small circular cottages, belonging to her "wives." A TV aerial sprouts from her roof, showing the comfortable lifestyle, the mixture of past and present, African tribalism and Western convenience.

When asked if she can really make rain her answer is simple. "Yes, if God wills."

South African women

The story of the on-going dynasty of the truly tribal African Rain Queen in a rapidly industrializing society shows clearly the complex issues women face in South Africa.

Women in all sections of society have to juggle with differing values and expectations. In one hand they hold spiritual and cultural values which could be Western European, Moslem, Hindu or African. In the other hand they hold the harsh realities of a fast-growing, Western, industrializing society. Their task is to create a balanced life for themselves and their families. And for the country as well.

chapter two

Milestones

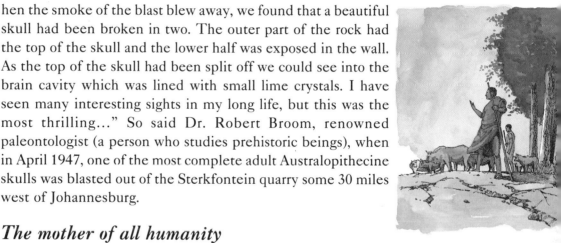

"**W**hen the smoke of the blast blew away, we found that a beautiful skull had been broken in two. The outer part of the rock had the top of the skull and the lower half was exposed in the wall. As the top of the skull had been split off we could see into the brain cavity which was lined with small lime crystals. I have seen many interesting sights in my long life, but this was the most thrilling..." So said Dr. Robert Broom, renowned paleontologist (a person who studies prehistoric beings), when in April 1947, one of the most complete adult Australopithecine skulls was blasted out of the Sterkfontein quarry some 30 miles west of Johannesburg.

The mother of all humanity

Khoisan woman (*opposite*) and Khoikhoi men (*right*). The Khoisan, or Bushmen, and the Khoikhoi were the earliest known people in the region which is present-day South Africa.

Mrs. Ples, short for Plesianthropus Transvaalensis, lived about a million years ago, walked on her hind legs and had a body that must have been practically human. The teeth sockets indicate she was a woman and the sutures, or seams, on the top of the skull, being closed, indicate the lady was getting on in years. Her brain was small, but she did have a form of speech.

If she was the forerunner of the human race, as many paleontologists believe, South Africa may well claim to be the cradle of the world and Mrs. Ples the mother of all humanity.

Contrasting land

When the very first Westerners, the Portuguese, sailed around the tip of the great African continent in the 15th century, they were circumnavigating a land of enormous diversity. In the east there were lush rolling grasslands, bush and forests, mountains, streams and even lakes and swamps. In the west, however, the earth was baked dry by furnace-like skies, fanned by desert winds, and sometimes threaded with rivers, frequently dried by the droughts. The huge central plateau, perched atop a dramatic mountain range, was mostly a treeless savannah, hot in summer and cold in winter. Today the geography is much the same, save for massive urbanization and extensive industrialization.

Once a permanent settlement was established on the southern tip of the continent by the Dutch in 1652, many hundreds of ships—Dutch, French, British, Portuguese—called on this coastline for fresh water, firewood, and food. They came into contact with the earliest known people of this region, the Khoisan, or Bushmen, and the Khoikhoi, sometimes also called the Hottentots.

The Bushmen

The Khoisan, a hunter-gatherer people, lived in total harmony with nature, feeding solely off the bounties of the veld (pronounced "felt"), or countryside. To do this they wandered far and wide across the land in groups consisting of a number of families, sometimes bigger when food was plentiful, breaking into smaller groups in times of scarcity.

The family unit was of utmost importance to their social and economic existence, and consisted of husband, wife or wives, and children. The husband and wives shared in the managing of the household. The domestic tasks and industries were carefully divided between them according to a custom refined over thousands of years of nomadic life.

Being nomadic they did not build permanent homes, but used rock shelters and caves as temporary dwellings, or built rough bush huts which could be quickly and easily assembled and taken down. The women were responsible for erecting these semi-

The distribution of the African tribes and European settlers in southern Africa at the beginning of the 19th century. The Dutch and English were still concentrated at the Cape then.

circular shelters of branches planted in the ground and covered with grass, and for keeping the camps clean and neat. They made hollows in the sand inside the shelters to sleep in and filled them with soft grass.

Because they were also responsible for fetching that precious commodity, water, they tried to ensure the dwellings were only an hour or two's walk from a water hole. Women were also responsible for collecting firewood and for making the fire and keeping it burning.

Gathering of food The prime concern of these hunter-gatherer people was the collection of food. The women and older children were responsible for the bulk of the family's food, collecting roots, fruits, shellfish and small, slow-moving game like tortoises. The men hunted larger prey with only a bow and poisoned arrow and an incredible fleetness of foot to assist them.

Men were responsible for making clothes for themselves and the women and children. They consisted of skin aprons tied around the waist with a hide thong. Married women also wore a large *kaross* ("ka-ROS"), a cloak made of animal skin tied in such a way that it could be used to carry a baby, the ostrich egg shells used for carrying water, and the food they collected.

Women, children and young men adorned themselves with ornaments.

The women would make beads out of ostrich egg shells to wear in their hair or as necklaces and bracelets. Leather and bark were used to make arm and leg bands.

Sadly, only a very few of these people exist today. Their resistance to the overrunning and occupation of their hunting grounds by settlers resulted in long and bitter clashes—and their near extinction, as thousands of men were killed and women and children were taken as servants or slaves. The migration of the Bantu tribes also put pressure on them and their hunting grounds. A few still live in the traditional way, but most have settled on farms or in reserves created for them.

Bushman women working at handicrafts. As much of their hunting ground has been taken over for farming and other uses, Bushmen today have to turn to other means of making a living, like selling their handicrafts.

Historical chronology

1100–1650 A.D.	Khoisan hunter-gatherers and nomadic farmers are spread across the country. African farmers grow in number and expand their territory.
1652	Jan van Riebeeck sets up a Dutch base at the Cape.
1658	Dutch East India Company brings the first slaves from the East Indies to the Cape.
1688	French Huguenot settlers arrive to join the Dutch and German families already farming at the Cape.
1806	British colonization begins as they take the Cape from the Dutch.
1815–35	The great African upheaval and migration takes place.
1834	British government abolishes slavery.
1835–41	The Great Trek takes thousands of Boer farmers, mainly of Dutch descent, into the interior of the country.
1853	Cape Colony gains its own elected government. The right to vote is based on property ownership.
1867	Discovery of diamonds at Kimberley.
1886	Discovery of gold near where Johannesburg stands today.
1879–81	The British army attacks and defeats the Zulus and then the Pedi, bringing to an end the independence of most Africans in South Africa.
1913	The Land Act ends the rights of Africans to own land outside the reserves, later to be called the homelands.
1948	The conservative Nationalist government comes into power and the implementation of legislated apartheid begins.
1960	The African National Congress is forced into exile.
1960	Police shoot and kill 26 black anti-pass law demonstrators at Sharpeville. The ANC changes from passive resistance to violence.
1976–77	Student riots lead to the deaths of hundreds of black youths.
1984–87	Frequent political disturbances lead the government to declare a state of emergency. Extensive world pressure is brought against the government for its policy of apartheid.
1989	The government releases the ANC leaders Nelson Mandela and Walter Sisulu from jail. This is the start of negotiations for a democratic government.
1992	The government calls a referendum to get a mandate from its white voters to continue the reform process for a non-racial democracy. In a very high voter turnout (85%), 68% voted in favor of reform.

The early Cape Colored community

In the 17th century many of the Khoikhoi mixed with and married the early Dutch sailors and now form what is today the Cape Colored community. At the same time Malay women were brought to the Cape as wives for Dutch sailors and settlers, and their cultural heritage was also added to the Cape Colored community. There is now a strong Moslem following and some of the women wear the traditional religious dress.

The Bantu tribes

The Bantu tribes of southern Africa form the biggest group in the region by far. The main subdivisions are the Swazi, Zulu and the Xhosa ("KHO-sa"), forming the greater Nguni ("n-GU-ni") tribe. The next biggest are the Sotho people which include the Tswana ("ts-WA-na"). In historical times these groups of people lived by a combination of farming and cattle raising.

In the Bantu family the father was chief and master of the household. The family was patrilineal, meaning heritage was passed down from father to son. The male role was to wage war, and in times of peace to take care of the herds of cattle, hunt, clear land for agriculture, and sometimes build huts for the family to live in. The women were expected to keep the home fires burning.

A Malay wedding. Malay women were brought over to the Cape as wives for Dutch sailors, and the men as slaves. They are today part of the Cape Colored community.

The woman's task in a Bantu family was extremely hard. She woke at sunrise to light the fire and warm the *mealie pap* (corn porridge) left from the evening meal. She would also prepare a small pot of fresh peanut sauce for the family's morning meal. She then went to the fields to plow, till or harvest. In the heat of the day she returned to prepare the evening meal. After that she saw to any other domestic chores like cleaning and washing. It was also her responsibility to collect firewood and greens like wild spinach from the veld.

Below right: Preparing food. The Bantu woman is mother, housekeeper, farmer and tradeswoman, all rolled into one.

A *woman's role* Although women were held in a subordinate position to men, they played a most important role in the life of the family as well as the tribe. In early tribal society, the law made little distinction between men and women, other than to give greater protection to women, punishing men more severely for injuries to women. In domestic affairs the woman took first place and she could take part in professional practices like divination, healing or magic.

The *bride price* The system of bride-price, or *lobola*—a number of cattle that had to be paid by a prospective husband to his bride-to-be's parents—ensured that marital duties on both sides were carried out. In historical times it certainly did not imply the woman was a bought chattel. She retained her own family name and could not be divorced unless she failed in her duties. In return, she could not divorce her husband unless he failed in his duties to her.

In all Bantu tribes love and respect of a mother was held up to young men as one of the highest virtues, and it was believed that a boy who was disrespectful to his mother did not have much hope of peace in this world or the next. However, this did not prevent Bantu women from having to work extremely hard, while their men, once they were no longer preoccupied with wars, could be found basking in the sun, smoking and gossiping.

A *woman's duties* Women were responsible for gathering wood and fetching water, which were often scarce commodities. Rearing the children was also left to the mothers and sometimes the older daughters, as was all

agriculture. Women cultivated sorghum, millet, beans, peanuts, and various vegetables. Corn, originally from South America, also became part of their diet by the 16th century. Women harvested the crops, and if there was a little extra food to sell or barter, the women kept the profits—usually to be used to the family's benefit. Girls were entrusted with "women's work" from a very early age. Most often women were not responsible for building their huts, but certainly had to clean them and maintain the dried mud walls, thatched roofs and cow dung floors.

Today the Bantu woman is still the backbone of southern Africa's rural development, but an equally large and increasing number now live and work in the urban areas.

Nandi, mother of the great king Shaka

In October 1827, while Shaka, the greatest warrior king of the Zulus, was on a hunting expedition, he heard that his mother, Nandi, had fallen ill. Immediately Shaka and H.F. Fynn, a trader well-versed in medicine, returned to the royal kraal. On arrival, they found she had contracted terminal dysentery. Nandi died only a few hours after their arrival.

Very moved by his mother's death, Shaka ordered a period of frantic mourning. In the frenzy whipped up as hundreds of thousands of Zulus lamented, a general massacre happened and thousands died. Some accounts hold that Shaka ordered the massacre of all those who did not lament loudly enough.

On the third day after her death, Nandi was buried in the hut where she had died, and it is said 10 of her servants "with limbs broken, as was the custom, were buried alive with her." An entire regiment of 12,000 warriors was ordered to guard her grave for a year. During the year following her death, the Zulu people were assembled three times for vast official mourning ceremonies.

Shaka was born unwanted and out of wedlock, something frowned upon by the Zulus of the time. His mother, Nandi (The Sweet One), the daughter of a neighboring Langeni tribal chief, became the third wife of Shaka's father, Senzangakona (The Rightful Doer), a chieftain of one of the Zulu clans. Although his mother tried to protect him, telling him he would one day be the greatest leader of his tribe, the child was not allowed to forget the unfortunate circumstances of his birth.

Shaka was totally devoted to his mother throughout his life and treated her as a surrogate wife, confessor, confidante and companion, as well as a mother. When Shaka became king, she lived at his royal kraal, and became the queen mother, known as the Great She-Elephant, a Zulu honorific. It is said she tried to restrict his ruthless warfare against neighboring tribes, but was unsuccessful, as she was in her attempts to persuade him to marry.

Nongquasi and the great Xhosa cattle killing

The terrain is rugged where the Gxarha River twists and plunges, drops down waterfalls and sometimes forms deep and mysterious pools, sometimes winds between precipitous cliffs. Here, in March 1856, near South Africa's Indian Ocean coast, a young orphan girl named Nongquasi ("non-KWA-si") went down to the river to fetch water from a deep pool. While there she saw men "who were different to ordinary men" and heard voices talking to her. Her uncle Mhlakaza ("m-SHLA-ka-za"), a renowned diviner who had interwoven Christianity with his own tribal beliefs of ancestor worship, acted as intermediary, interpreting Nongquasi's ghostly tales to the Xhosa nation.

"Tell the Xhosa people to kill all their cattle, destroy their crops and wait for a miracle," the spirits told Nongquasi. Beautiful cattle would appear in the thousands, the grain pits would fill to overflowing, an abundance of their other desires—guns, wagons, clothes—would be given to them, and a great wind would sweep all the whites and any unbelieving blacks into the sea. So said the spirits.

Conditions were ripe for the tribal people to believe this prophecy: Ancestor worship was strong among the Xhosa people; the British colonialists were fast eroding the Xhosa land, winning the wars and skirmishes more and more, often due to their superior weapons—guns; and a devastating and contagious lung sickness was sweeping through their precious herds of cattle, killing many. The Xhosa nation was at the end of its tether. The prophecy seemed like a god-given sign that their suffering was soon to be over. (Picture shows an unequal battle between the British and the tribesmen.)

After many of the chiefs had consulted with Nongquasi through her interpreter uncle, they believed the spirits of the ancestors had returned to advise them. Over 200,000 cattle were killed, crops were consumed or destroyed. The prophecy due to take place on February 18, 1857 was not fulfilled and tens of thousands of Xhosa died of starvation.

The Dutch at the Cape in the 1700s. By then some of the African tribal people were working in the European settlements as laborers.

The mass migrations

In the late 1600s a number of French Huguenots, who were Calvinists, immigrated to the Cape to escape religious persecution in their homeland at the hand of King Louis XIV. They joined the Dutch immigrants who had been at the Cape for some 50 years.

Soon these settlers (the Dutch and the French) needed more land. They expanded east, up the coast toward the city now called Port Elizabeth. This move clashed with the expansion and migrations of the Bantu tribes, who were moving southwest from the Natal coast toward the southern Cape. The population increase of all the different groups in southern Africa during the late 18th and early 19th centuries led to pressures that eventually gave rise to the joining of the Zulu tribes into a major fighting force under their leader, Shaka. The effects on the people in this southern African region were severe, leading to wars, mass migrations, and tremendous hardship.

Mmanthasisi leads her people At this time a great woman leader rose to power among the Tlokwa ("TLO-kwa"), a Sotho tribe who lived on the central plateau in the region of current-day Lesotho. Mmanthasisi ("man-ta-SI-si"), born in 1781, gained a reputation for her ferocity and plundering ways as she led her people during this tumultuous period, sometimes in war and sometimes in search of grazing for the cattle and land on which to grow food. Under her leadership, until her death in 1835, the Tlokwa were feared as a formidable force.

Early European settlers

In 1820 nearly 5,000 British immigrants landed at the Cape Colony where Port Elizabeth is today, having been promised portions of land to farm. However, they had not been told how harsh and very different the farming conditions were compared to their homeland. Nor were they told that their farms were on the frontier, and they would effectively be the buffer between the Colony and the Xhosa tribes. The battle between the two groups for land led to a number of wars.

Making their mark Despite many years of poverty and hardship, these immigrants made their way as farmers, traders and craftsmen and have been praised for their contributions to the entire country. Called the 1820 Settlers, they played a major role in the administration of the Cape as the British style of governing changed from despotic colonial power to a more representative system in the 1850s. British influence was strong not only in government, law and administration, but also in the broader social and cultural sense. Towns and villages had a higher concentration of English-speaking people, while the Afrikaners (people of Dutch descent), although greater in number, were mostly rural people. The rural-urban balance between the two groups is fairly similar today.

Few Settler women left the home to work for a living, especially as there were not many professions considered suitable for women of the time. However, being a plumassier—working in ornamental ostrich feathers—certainly was acceptable. Strangely, as early as 1854 there were gadgets on the market to lighten the burden of domestic work. A type of "family washing machine" was advertised, which when the handle was turned, rubbed the clothes around the roller and so washed them.

Differences The more liberal nature of the 1820 Settlers has often caused a divide between the two groups of white South African women (the English-speaking women of British descent and the Afrikaans-speaking women who originated from the early Dutch settlers). In recent times English-speaking women have more often been involved in leading feminist thought in South Africa.

One of the headmistresses who left the United Kingdom to establish a school for the Settler families had very modern intentions for the time as she wanted to "educate women that they shall be emancipated and placed on an equality with men—that they may be thoroughly independent of them..."

Indians join the cultural melting pot

In the mid-19th century the pioneering European sugarcane planters felt they needed labor skilled in this form of agriculture. They were given permission to recruit workers from the Indian sub-continent. So in 1860, 340 Indians—197 men, 89 women and 54 children—arrived in Natal, where the sugarcane grew in the sub-tropical climate. Most of these first immigrants were Hindus, but there were also a number of Moslems, Christians and other groups among the arrivals. Although imported primarily to work on the sugarcane plantations, they had many skills and soon a number were absorbed into other businesses.

Over the next five decades some 150,000 Indians were attracted by the prospects of trade in the new colony and emigrated to South Africa. Most of them came to the country under contract and were indentured, or enslaved, to their employers for periods of at least three years before they could be free to work as they pleased.

Indians today Although the majority of the Indian population still lives in Durban and other areas of Natal, they have also spread throughout the country. They live mainly in urban areas, where they are successfully involved in trading, business and commerce, as well as in

Indians arrived in South Africa in the mid-1800s to work on the sugarcane plantations. To this day they have clung to their traditions, but changes are also in the air. This is Fatima Meer, one of a growing group of feminists and politcial activists among the Indian community.

the professions. Today South Africa's Indian population numbers about a million with 65% being Hindus, 20% Moslems and the rest mainly Christians and Buddhists.

At first women played a traditional role of homemaker, wife, and mother. In the early years of their settlement in the country, girls were often not allowed to attend school at all. Slowly this attitude changed, and today a significant and growing number of women go to college and hold their own in business and the professions.

South Africa's Great Trek

The Great Trek, the first mass migration of immigrant South Africans, began in 1835 and did not end till 1854. Afrikaner frontier farmers, descendants of the Dutch who had come to establish a halfway station for their trading empire, as well as the French Huguenots who had left Europe to escape religious persecution, had moved into the hinterland from the settlement now known as Cape Town.

An independent people, as is the nature of pioneers, they found life under British rule intolerable. The Afrikaners were Christians and considered the African tribes in the area heathens—a vast difference, they felt. Thus the official British policy of equality in church and state was unacceptable to them and they decided to trek into the interior, an area uncharted and quite unknown to them.

Carrying all their possessions in their ox-drawn wagons, a number of different groups set off, some going northward to what is today called the Orange Free State province, and even further to the Transvaal province. A few even crossed the great Limpopo River. Others went north and then eastward, toward what is today called Durban. The journeys were arduous and dangerous. The tribal inhabitants of the land tried to keep them at bay and battles and skirmishes were frequent. Lives were also lost by attacks from wild animals. Many of the Voortrekkers or Boers, as they were called, died from diseases like malaria, blackwater and sleeping sickness which is carried by the tsetse fly in some areas.

It was no easy task pulling wagons up and down the steep Drakensberg mountain range, which at its highest rises some 11,000 feet. At times the wheels had to be taken off and carried up these precipitous slopes. Continuously the women were at their men's sides, not only helping with the new tasks that confronted them with each new day, but also trying to keep the group's morale up despite the hardships they faced. They were also responsible for keeping the family units intact, fed and clothed, and the children educated to enable them all to read the Bible.

Voortrekker women

From about 1830 there was much talk in the Cape Colony among the Afrikaner farmers, a fiercely independent people, of getting away from what they saw as British misrule. After a number of north-bound reconnaissance trips, the Great Trek began in earnest in 1835. The Voortrekkers ("FOOR-trek-kers"), or Boers, formed into groups, loading their precious possessions onto ox-drawn wagons and heading into what was largely unknown territory. They had no intention of ever returning south again.

Having chosen the pioneering way of life beside their men on the eastern Cape border, many of the women who took part in the Great Trek were accustomed to facing danger and to living with very few, if any, home comforts. In fact, they were so thoroughly prepared that, far removed from settled civilization, they were still able to hold to their traditions in the midst of the untamed interior of the Dark Continent, as Africa was often called.

Battles and massacres Because the routes the Voortrekker groups took into the interior crossed the paths of the Bantu tribes at the time of their great upheaval, they were involved in a number of battles and bloody massacres. The Voortrekker woman made her presence felt as a powerful moral

influence, particularly in these moments of need as, in the heat of battle, she cast bullets, loaded guns and often fired on the enemy.

If her husband became ill, or worse, died (diseases like malaria or blackwater often wracked the Trekker groups, and snake and scorpion bites could also be deadly), a wife would take over and drive the wagon through uncharted, wild and dangerous regions. When they crossed the rugged Drakensberg mountain range, the women, on foot, had to help carry the heavy wagon wheels and other trek equipment up the rocky, precipitous slopes.

In the struggles with the natives, women were at the front with the men, loading guns, taking care of the wounded and giving moral support.

Providing for the family Much like her Bantu counterpart, the Voortrekker woman had to provide meals and a home life for her family regardless of rain, cold, the scarcity of firewood and all the other privations of living in a moving wagon.

She dressed or dried the meat, making biltong, baked the bread, griddle cakes and rusks, made her own soap using substances from the lye-bush and her own candles using the tallow dipping method or moulds to shape the candles. Wicks were made of twisted linen.

She was also the seamstress, responsible for the men's embroidered waistcoats and the large, intricate sun bonnets the women and girls used to keep the harsh African sun off their faces.

Importance of education The woman was responsible for the children's education, most importantly teaching them to read so they could study the Bible. Mothers also instilled the values of obedience, courtesy and faithfulness in their children as well as cleanliness and godliness. The Calvinist faith played a major role in their lives and family Bible readings were a daily occurrence.

Forced to be self-reliant, women nursed not only their own families, but others in the community too. In the absence of a physician they had to develop home remedies for the many ailments that affected their families along the route. A high number of babies died due to the lack of necessary medical attention, medicine and care. Magdalena Retief, wife of one of the most prominent Trekker leaders, Piet Retief, had 15 children, but by the time her husband was killed in a battle against the Zulus, only five of them were still alive.

Even more so than their men, the Voortrekker women could be commended for their resilience, self-sufficiency and dogged determination. They never lost their independent spirit so that even now a very large number of them live on outlying farms and maintain their staunch Calvinistic faith.

The nature of the Boers

By 1854 the Great Trek had come to an end with the British acceptance, albeit temporary, of the independence of their territories. Trekkers, who were also

Biltong is a type of dried, salted meat, similar to beef jerky. The meat, preferably game, is cut into thin strips, marinated in a mixture of spices, vinegar and salt, and then hung up in the sun to dry. In days before refrigeration it was the only way the Boers could preserve the meat from the game they shot. Today it has become a national delicacy and is usually eaten as a snack.

known as Boers, settled into an agrarian way of life.

Living on far-flung farms, the Boers had very little contact with the ideas and beliefs developing in the towns and villages, as well as the rest of the world, and their needs remained simple. It was said that a man would want in a wife a woman who could bear and rear his children, organize the servants, make his moleskin clothes and pour his coffee when he came home from the fields. She would be all the better catch if she brought some "equity" into the marriage—cattle, sheep and household goods were prized in those distant communities. She was also expected to be his financial advisor, both on the home front and in external business. In other words she would control the purse strings with his blessing. Finally he wanted someone who would save him from the weariness and solitude of living on the farm on his own.

A woman would want a husband capable of looking after the farm, who would father her children and never buy or sell anything without first asking her advice. A bonus would be an affectionate man who was not ill-tempered.

Since most of the men and women in the neighborhood would have been raised in similar conditions, they would usually meet these expectations, making the choice of a spouse quite simple.

Boer women exercised great influence over their men and their community, perhaps because of the enormous sacrifices they were always willing to make for their independence. (This can be seen in the women's role during the Great Trek and the Anglo-Boer War.)

Boer women were very important in the formation of the Afrikaner ethnic consciousness. Their roles as wives and mothers as well as initiators of organizations and as figures in the public arena were equally important. Today they still play a strong role in maintaining the group's cultural identity.

A Boer family reading the Bible together. Governed by a strict religion and isolated from the rest of the world on their remote farms, Boers became conservative and inward-looking.

An Afrikaner woman and her children at a commemoration of a Boer victory over the British during the war.

1899; and ended in Boer defeat in 1901. The division this war caused between the two groups is still sometimes evident in South Africa today.

During the war many women ran the farms on their own while their men were fighting and later when they were sent to prisoner-of-war camps in foreign countries. As part of a scorched earth policy, the British burned down many Boer homesteads and farms to prevent the guerrillas from getting help from their farming communities and especially their defiant womenfolk. As a result many women and children were made homeless. To protect them, as well as the families of the men who had surrendered, the British decided to uproot almost an entire nation and place them in relief camps—which later became concentration camps. In one instance several hundred women and children were loaded into open railway cars and sent off to a camp many hundreds of miles away.

A champion of the Boers A heroine of the Boer War, Marie Koopmans-de Wet was proud of her Dutch ancestry, and although she lived in Cape Town, had a keen interest in the Boer republics.

With the onset of the war, she organized a peace petition with over 16,000 signatures which was sent to Britain's Queen Victoria. Sadly the war worsened. Marie rallied the support of her fellow Capetonians, many of whom

The Anglo-Boer War

The Anglo-Boer War between the British government, which controlled the Natal and Cape areas, and the two independent Boer republics, began in were of British descent, and used her home as a collection point for clothes and supplies for the women and children in the concentration camps. Her efforts led to her being placed under house arrest by the British. This meant she was not allowed to leave her home at all, but, undaunted, she continued her work for two years after the end of the war.

This experience made her realize the need for women's organizations and she helped found the Afrikaans Christian Women's Organization.

Disease and death in the camps

Once rumors reached the United Kingdom about the bad conditions in the refugee camps, a courageous young British woman, Emily Hobhouse, set off for the war zone. She visited 34 of the camps and was horrified by what she encountered, horrified that human beings could be kept in such appalling conditions. Disease was rife, and at times women and children died by the hundreds from typhoid and measles. People were sleeping on the ground because there was no furniture in the camps. There was also a severe shortage of food. Although drinking water from the rivers needed to be boiled to prevent the spread of disease, they had no utensils to boil the water in and no fuel for the fires.

Emily worked ceaselessly, sharing what clothes and food she could buy with money from a distress fund she had set up in England. But the situation got steadily worse as more and more prisoners arrived. In 1901, within three months, some 4,067 people—3,245 of them children—died in one camp near the city of Bloemfontein.

Emily returned to England to publicize what she had discovered and eventually managed to force the British government to improve conditions. After the war she returned to South Africa to implement a scheme to help women earn a living so they could eventually afford to return to their farms. She started a weaving school for girls and young women and within three years had developed 24 others. She then persuaded the government to take over their management, after which she returned to England.

A Boer tribute

So grateful were the Boers to this Englishwoman that, despite the enormous amount of antagonism they felt toward her nation, they invited her to unveil the National Women's Monument in honor of the 26,000 women and children who had died in the concentration camps. Unfortunately ill health prevented this, but when she died her ashes were buried at the foot of the monument—a Boer tribute to this Englishwoman.

Struggle for the vote

Although the first claim for the right for women to vote in South Africa was made before most of the rest of the world had begun suffrage (the right to vote) movements, the vast majority of women still have no right to vote. That is because the apartheid government system did not give the vote to any black people. This is about to change as the new constitution takes shape.

In 1843 a group of Voortrekker women in Pietermaritzburg, Natal, staked their claim to the vote. A spokeswoman stated to the British High Commissioner who governed the territory, that as they had taken part in various battles alongside their husbands, they had been promised the right to a voice in all matters concerning the state of the country. However, the claim was dismissed by the High Commissioner, who later said, "I endeavored to impress on them that such a liberty as they seemed to dream of had never been recognized in any civil society. That I regretted that as married ladies they boasted of a freedom that even in a social state they could not claim...and that I considered it a disgrace on their husbands to allow such a state of freedom."

Unfortunately this first burst of emancipation was not followed up by the Afrikaner women for well over 70 years despite the fact that throughout their early history they had exercised a great influence within their community.

A lot of the blame for this has been laid at the feet of their stern Calvinist faith, manifest in the Dutch Reformed Church, which developed with the Afrikaner nation. Strong opposition to women voting came from the many men in the church, including C.J. Langenhoven, a noted Afrikaner academic of the time. He claimed that special capacities had been allotted to different groups of people: the use of the head was reserved for white men, the hand for black men and the heart for all women. He argued that the head alone could concern itself with political matters!

No easy task When women began to campaign actively for the right to vote at the beginning of this century, the movement was led in the most part by urban women. At first the rural Afrikaner women did not support the movement. This slowed down its achievements a lot, and the men in politics were able to greet the demands with a mixture of amusement, derision, hostility and indifference. In 1899 a Private Members Bill was introduced in the Cape Legislature seeking the vote for women, but was laughed out of court, with the loudest and most scornful laughter coming from a leading politician, John X. Merriman.

Celebrating International Women's Day on March 8, 1991. Sadly, unlike many of their sisters in the rest of the world, black women in South Africa did not have the vote at this stage. However, things are changing. In a referendum in March 1992, white South Africans voted in favor of reforms toward a non racial democracy.

A national organization is formed In Natal women suffragettes at first had as little success as their Cape counterparts. The first movement, the Women's Enfranchise League, founded in Durban in 1902, was widespread throughout the country by 1911. However, when Emmeline Pankhurst, the leader of British suffragettes, visited this seaside city, the *Natal Mercury* newspaper wrote: "We hope that women suffragists have enjoyed their picnic in Durban, but we do not think the political effort of their visit can have rewarded their endeavours, and we cannot pretend that we have any regret for their non-success."

This was the biggest and most important suffragette body, and was also the only national body. Its members were mostly English-speaking, urban women who, with a high degree of courage, initiative and dedication, faced a largely hostile or unconcerned public, especially in the early years.

Eventually, in 1930, white South African women were granted the vote.

In spite of earlier promises, Colored women were excluded, although at that stage their men still had the vote. It was a non-victorious victory, as was so aptly summed up in the words of feminist writer Olive Schreiner's husband: "An act that remedied an injustice against part of a sex by perpetrating racism was not a victory at all."

Mining gold. The discovery of gold in 1886 led to the urbanization and industrialization of South Africa.

Women demand their rights in the workplace

The growth of the suffrage movement did not take place in a vacuum. Demanding the vote and eventually winning it—for some—was linked to changes taking place in the position of women in society at that time. In the early years of the country's urban development many women were legally, economically and socially dependent on their male relatives. But by 1930 much of this had changed. Industrialization meant increasing numbers of women were working outside the home and earning a wage, making them much more independent. The effect of this is summed up by the actions of Edith Woods, a schoolteacher, who, in 1923, was summoned to court for refusing to pay her taxes. Her defense: taxing a person without allowing the person government representation is tyrannical.

The discovery of gold in the Transvaal in 1886 changed the face of South Africa. Very soon the mining town now known as Johannesburg, or Egoli as many Africans call it, sprang up. Urbanization and industrialization were kick-started into action as towns developed around the many mines all along the gold reef.

A feisty first In the first decade of this century the country saw an upsurge of socialist and trade union activity in line with movements in the industrializing world of the time. As the number of factories grew in South Africa, so the number of women in the work force increased. Their participation in working class struggles dates back to their involvement in the Industrial and Commercial Workers Union and the Women Workers General Union of the '20s. Mary Fitzgerald, a tiny, feisty, Irish immigrant, helped organize two tram strikes in 1911. She was the first woman in the country to become involved in trade union work.

As a typist for the Mine Workers Union she saw the miners' very bad

work conditions: numerous fatal accidents, no compensation for the deceased's family, and a high incidence of the dreaded lung disease, phthisis. She attended meetings and soon had thousands of followers, especially with her involvement in the miners' and general strikes of 1913 and 1914 where, shouting defiance at the police, she encouraged miners to stand firm.

In the '30s many people moved into the towns as industry grew. The Depression years also led to an influx of rural people no longer able to make a living on their farms. A fairly high number of white and Colored women, as well as African men, worked in the semi- and unskilled jobs in factories, leaving domestic work to the African women. In this period the garment and textiles unions became a force to be reckoned with under the strong leadership of women like Johanna and Hester Cornelius, Anna Scheepers and Dulcie Hartwell. Under their leadership, thousands of white and Colored women went out on strike to try to stave off wage cuts during the Depression years, and to demand improved working conditions.

Members of the South African Clothing and Textiles Workers Union showing their solidarity. South African women have been in the forefront of the trade union movement since the 1920s.

African women's movement There were very few African women in the factories until the '60s when Lucy Mvubelo ("mm-VU-bay-lo") and Sarah Chitja ("CHI-cha") steered the largest African union in the country, the National Union of Clothing Workers. In the late '70s women's militancy rose again as high inflation made a mockery of the very low wages they were earning. Other issues brought up during these strikes were the poor working conditions and the way grievances were dealt with.

As the decades progressed and the racial discrimination caused by the apartheid laws took root, the role of women in society became more politicized, especially that of the urban black woman.

The Women's League of the African National Congress was founded in 1948. In 1954 the Federation of South African Women, a non-racial body, was set up to fight for women's rights. It was also committed to the struggle against apartheid. The Federation played a prominent part in the passive resistance movements in the '50s and led the massive anti-pass demonstration in August 1956.

As part of its apartheid policy the Nationalist government announced in 1955 that African women had to carry passes, an identity document giving full details, such as place of birth, residence and so on. Since 1913 various governments had tried to force women to carry these documents, but without success. Men had been forced to carry passes many years earlier.

Massive rallies were held all over the country, the most famous being in August 1956. Over 20,000 women from all over South Africa gathered in front of the government buildings in Pretoria and sang in Zulu, "Strijdom [then Prime Minister], you have struck a rock—you have tampered with the women."

It took the government a further seven years before they dared to enforce the pass laws on African women.

A poster which registers the protest of the people againt the pass laws.

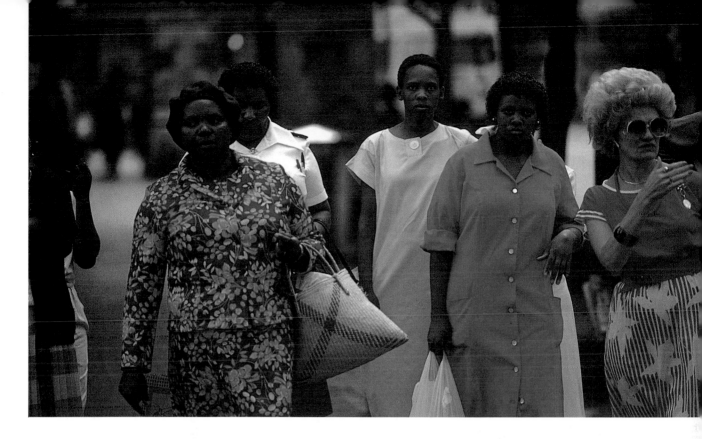

Professional women Although a fairly high number of white women have chosen to be homemakers (not too strenuous a task as many are able to afford full-time domestic help), the role of professional working women has become more important to the economy.

This was first felt in the boom years of the '70s and early '80s when demand outstripped the supply of skilled professionals. It was felt again when many professionals emigrated to escape the more recent civil unrest, causing a shortfall. More and more professional working women have their feet in the door, but the battle against sexual—and in the case of black women, color—discrimination is far from over.

Where to the future Women have played an extensive role in shaping the history of the land, from Mrs. Ples as she looked out of her cave a million and a half years ago, to the strong and determined African and European-settler women who migrated through the untamed interior, to the women who were part of an early industrializing labor force.

Various women from different groups chipping away in many different ways helped lead to the ending of the apartheid system in 1990. With the chance to draw up a new constitution, it is up to South Africa's millions of women from every walk of life to see that equality is written into their future, and that of their country.

South African women today. Their destiny is in their own hands.

chapter three

Women in Society

The contributions women have made to the South African society have been as varied as the diverse population, as dramatic as the country's tumultuous social and political history. And like almost all countries both African and Western—South Africa being a mixture of both—men have dominated the scene, making it necessary for women not only to strive to reach the top in their fields, but to struggle against male domination and, for some, racial discrimination as well. Today many women of all colors and creeds hold their own in most every field.

The apartheid system has at once made life complex, unfair and even unbearable for many, but it has also brought to the fore women's strength and compassion as many have rallied to help their less fortunate or more discriminated-against sisters. And they have chosen to do this through many different avenues.

Politics: *The fight for a just society*

Whether as domestic worker (*opposite*) or political activist like Sheena Duncan (*right*), women in South Africa contribute in no small way to the society they live in.

Although there have never been many women in the formal political arena, they entered it as soon as the restrictive legislation that barred them from official office was lifted. Mary Fitzgerald, better known as Pickhandle Mary, was one of three of the first women elected to the Johannesburg Town Council in 1915, the first time women were allowed to run for office or vote in municipal elections. Women were barred from voting in national elections until 1930.

Righting wrongs The prominent women in politics have almost all been altruistic, that is, committed to righting the wrongs of society, and in more recent times the wrongs brought about by the apartheid system. Some have worked from within Parliament, like Leila Reitz, the first woman in Parliament, and Margaret Ballinger, who followed close on her heals. Ballinger was also an active campaigner for women's and civil rights in the '20s, '30s and beyond. Bertha Solomon, one of the country's first women attorneys, became a Member of Parliament in 1938 in an attempt to improve women's legal rights. When Parliament was not in session, she balanced her lofty ideals with down-to-earth community work and ran soup kitchens for the very poor in her constituency.

Probably the most well-known woman in formal politics, Helen Suzman served in opposition to the apartheid government for 37 years. For much of that time she was the lone elected representative of her party. (She is profiled in Chapter 5.) With her probing questions to Parliament she kept local and world attention on the issues of South African human rights.

The local role Both black and white women have played a very important role in local politics, becoming town and city councillors and on many occasions mayors. Local government often offers a more immediate response to changes effected by councillors, which can be very rewarding. (Black South Africans

Championing politics and law

When Bertha Solomon married in 1913, she realized that she had lost certain important legal rights. She studied law, and became the second woman lawyer in the country once the barriers to women entering this profession were removed in 1923.

Bertha, who was born just before the turn of the century, devoted her life to trying to get political and legal rights for women. Without the vote, women were powerless to change their legal position. Women married "in community of property," which meant everything they owned became joint property, but a husband had the legal right to do what he liked with his wife's property. A wife, however, could not sign any legal contract without his written permission! This caused a lot of problems when many men were away fighting in World War II.

Backed by all the women's organizations of the time, she argued in Parliament for the Matrimonial Affairs Act, and in 1953, Bertha, an opposition member to the Nationalist government, had "her" Act passed, which severely limited a husband's rights in handling his wife's earnings and property.

Bertha continued to campaign for human rights until her death in 1969.

The relaunch of the ANC Women's League in 1990 after the ban on it was lifted. Black women could only fight for their rights outside of formal politics as they did not have the vote.

were barred from national politics.)

As local politics is much more community-based, women feel their contributions at this level have a more immediate and direct effect on people's quality of life.

Jacobeth Agnes Poo, a nurse since 1952, became the first woman mayor of Alexander township in 1989. She was moved to take up the challenge of this poor, black residential neighborhood alongside Johannesburg, despite the life-threatening violence and political unrest because "our housing situation can only be described as painful havoc." The suffering caused by a chronic housing shortage led to related problems like the outbreak of polio and measles, as well as rampant crime. She felt it her Christian duty to try and improve these conditions.

The crossover Molly Blackburn, killed in a car crash in 1985, entered formal politics as a city councillor determined to fight for a non-racial democratic country for all. Soon her courage, concern and selfless dedication to the underprivileged people of the poor and strife-torn region of eastern Cape allowed her to cross into the informal political arena as well, where she gained a huge following. This is evidenced by the thousands of black people who attended the funeral of a white woman who had devoted her life to improving theirs.

What is the ANC or African National Congress?

In the early 1900s black South Africans began to organize a resistance to white rule. Slowly the movement gathered strength, cutting across tribal lines, and finally the African National Congress was established in January 1913 with the headquarters in Johannesburg. (Picture below shows early ANC leaders.) The first president, Reverend John Dube, had studied in England, and early members of the ANC were African men who had obtained an eduction mainly through English-run mission schools. Many of these members had also been sent abroad by the missions for further education and training in various professions. The initial role of the ANC was to persuade the white government to recognize all people as equals.

Annual conferences were held, and in 1944 a Congress Youth League was formed. The movement quickly gained momentum when the Afrikaners took control of the government in 1948 and began to build rigid systems of apartheid.

Turn to violence

The ANC organized on-going passive resistance campaigns against the exclusion of black people from the process of government. Then in April 1960 the government banned the ANC, thus it was no longer a lawful political organization. With this act 50 years of non-violent struggle was brought to nothing, and by mid-1961 the ANC decided that to achieve its aims it would have to use violent methods of resistance. In 1961 Umkhonto we Sizwe ("OOM-kon-toe way SIS-wa"), or "the Spear of the Nation," the military wing of the ANC, was formed. Its tactics of sabotage were at first aimed at damaging only buildings and property, but avoiding loss of life.

In 1963 the top leaders of the ANC were brought to trial and sentenced to life imprisonment. The organization went into exile and continued its work. As the government laws became more repressive, the ANC again changed its tactics and civilians became targets of sabotage. Because of internal and external pressure, the figurehead and now the leader of the ANC, Nelson Mandela, and many other members were released from jail in February 1990. The ban on the organization has been lifted, and it once more operates as a political party in South Africa.

Opposing discrimination

Helen Joseph, committed to the principles of communism, has against all odds worked relentlessly to oppose discrimination and injustice. A warm, vivacious and intense woman, she was one of the founder-members of the powerful Federation of South African Women.

Despite bannings, house arrest and attacks on her home, she has remained in South Africa when she could have gone into exile in England where she was born. She was also a "listed person" for 36 years, which meant she could not be quoted in the press nor could she publish her works in South Africa. She was unlisted in 1990 at the age of 86. Several of her books have been published since then, including her autobiography, and she has been honored overseas.

Determined to fight for human rights
Many women in South Africa have been outraged because formal politics, and thus the vote, has in the main been denied to African, Asian and Colored people. Many have given up everything, some have even given their lives, to oppose an unjust government and fight for what is right and fair, a future of equality for their children.

Through all the decades of apartheid rule Nontsikelelo ("non-SI-KI-lay-lo") Albertina Sisulu has been a guiding and fearless light to millions of women struggling with daily life under an unjust system. (She is profiled in Chapter 5.) Often called "The Mother of the Nation," Albertina, who has been jailed, banned, placed under house arrest and more, has continued to organize women's voices, mainly through the Federation of South African Women.

There are others: the courageous women of the Black Sash, who draw public attention to issues with silent demonstrations, but who also run advice offices throughout the country to help people caught in the web of apartheid laws; Helen Joseph, a living symbol of hope to many, particularly those whites who are sincerely committed to a just and peaceful non-racial southern Africa; Frene Ginwala, a member of the ANC Women's League task force, a lawyer, historian, journalist and committed fighter for women's rights.

to be a missionary. However, once differentiated education was introduced for children of different races, she walked out of the formal teaching profession, never to return. By this time she had married a newly qualified doctor and set up home in Soweto.

In 1968 she became president of the African Housewives' League, which brought her into daily contact with Soweto's women whose everyday needs and problems became her concern. It was in trying to voice the frustrations of her people that she was harassed and jailed. As child care is one of the most pressing issues for working women, she says her wish is that women of all races would come together and find a solution for the care of all children in South Africa. She feels that if women do not plan now they will be leaving their children no heritage.

Protesting the VAT tax. Sally Motlana is on Vatwatch, the consumer watchdog set up after the VAT tax was introduced, to protect consumers from retailers who may use the tax to overcharge.

The line is smudged For many women the dividing line between politics and social welfare, or caring for the community, is smudged or may not even exist at all. A civic leader like Sally Motlana in Soweto is just such a woman. Her involvement in the community and especially in the plight of urban black women has led her into politics (and because of her convictions, to jail as well), into broad-based consumer issues and into religious administration.

Sally began life as a schoolteacher, although she says her passion was always

Western ways Sally's religious involvement extended to becoming the vice chairperson of the South African Council of Churches, but it did not stop her strong opposition to the churches' recognition of tribal marriage, as she feels it perpetuates the inferior status of women. She has also attacked the custom of polygamy which allows African men to take more than one wife, saying that it is quite unacceptable to the woman of today who is sophisticated, educated and subscribes to Western standards.

Winnie Mandela

Winifred Madikizela married Nelson Mandela at her family village in the Transkei in 1958—a 22-year-old bride. The romance began when Winnie watched a tall, imposing lawyer defend one of her girlfriends in court. Later she was introduced to him by mutual friends. The relationship bloomed, but even in those early days she felt he belonged to everyone. She once said, "Life with Nelson was life without him." Little did she know how prophetic this would be.

Early years

Winnie's father was a primary school principal and her mother a domestic science teacher. Born in 1936, Winnie grew up in a large extended family, which helped to cushion the blow of her mother's early death. When she was 16, she moved to Johannesburg to train as a medical social worker. She graduated with an award for best student and became the first black medical social worker at one of the biggest hospitals in the country. At this time she also attended political meetings and took part in acts of non-violent resistance.

Winnie and Nelson had two daughters, Zenani and Zindziswa, but they did not see very much of each other as he was very involved with the ANC. The treason trial where he was one of the accused was also underway. In 1963 Nelson was given a life sentence.

Although her home life was now shattered, Winnie continued her political activities. She was detained without trial for 491 days as the authorities tried to make her reveal information about the ANC. She was then given a banning order, meaning she was restricted in what she could do and where she could go, and had to remain in her home at nights and on weekends. This was almost continuous for 13 years. After the student uprisings in 1976 against the government, Winnie was banished to Brandfort, a desolate, poverty-stricken rural area. There she set up a nursery school and a clinic to help the community.

Mandela United Football Club

When her home in Brandfort was firebombed, she returned to Soweto, near Johannesburg. She continued in the political struggle, especially during the political uprisings of the '80s, becoming a major leader in her own right.

However, her brutal treatment at the hands of the authorities all her adult life, coupled with her own excessive self-esteem, led her to form the Mandela United Football Club in 1986. This group of youths became her bodyguard. Sadly three former club members have been convicted of murder and in 1991 Winnie was found guilty of "conspiracy to kidnap and of having acted as an accessory to assault." She was sentenced to six years in jail, but she was released on bail as the case is on appeal.

In February 1990 she was reunited with her husband after 27 years when he was released from jail. In 1992 Winnie and Nelson separated.

Social work: Care and concern for the community

Many women from all walks of life have always played an important role in the welfare services, schools, day care centers, clinics, medical institutions and charities. Today, as barriers and prejudices slowly fall away, it is expected that even more women will participate at all levels in the communities.

Although the government has given much larger sums of money to all sections of social welfare in recent years, the discriminatory welfare system of the past meant a great many non-governmental organizations, or NGOs, were formed throughout the country to help relieve the hardships of the underprivileged. They were mainly founded, formed and run by women.

Drive against rural hunger and poverty
In 1980 many voluntary organizations felt there was a need to coordinate action on rural hunger and poverty. Operation Hunger emerged and at the helm was the indomitable Ina Perlman. Their objectives were twofold: to feed hundreds of thousands of starving children and in the long term to develop self-help projects in these poor communities. With Ina's never-ending energy and drive, Operation Hunger grew to be a massive umbrella body that raises millions of dollars each year in donations both at home and overseas and ensures the money is spent on the needy.

Today O. H., as it is often called, also has a large wing of self-help development projects where communities, at their own request, are assisted in using their skills and land to generate food for the families at first, and then, an income and a life without poverty. A large majority of the participants in these projects are women. Ina Perlman and her dedicated staff are responsible for thriving communities where once there was nothing but famine.

Silent vigil In 1955 rows of women, each with a black sash across one shoulder, stood silent vigil outside

Operation Hunger volunteers go on the street to publicize their projects and ask for donations.

Parliament. They also held country-wide meetings, marches and demonstrations wherever cabinet ministers were making public appearances and submitted petitions to the government. They were not affiliated with any political party, but their outrage was unanimous. It was directed against the removal of the Colored men from the common voters role by the apartheid government—the beginning of institutionalized racism. They called their organization the Women's Defence of the Constitution League, but soon became known as the Black Sash.

An all-women's organization—men can be affiliate members—the Black Sash maintains much the same stance today. They hold silent vigils which often invoke extreme ire from the public, particularly white men who harass the women, jeer and curse at them and have been known to use long hat pins on them too. Although still not affiliated with any political party, they take an active part in socio-political issues. They also run a number of advice bureaus in urban areas for people caught in the web of apartheid law.

As President Sheena Duncan once said, "We thought we were going to change the history of South Africa..." Single-handed that was not to be, but each contribution of those women adds to the overall uplifting of at least some of the people. Black Sash was

Members of the Black Sash in a protest march in the township of Soweto.

nominated for the Nobel Peace Prize in 1987.

A new start for children A most dedicated and concerned woman, Maggie Nkwe ("NN-kway") saw the desperate need for a home in Soweto for abandoned children. She has devoted her life to the formation and running of Orlando Children's Home, an organization that has given hundreds of children a start in life—children who might otherwise have never experienced love of any sort, perhaps might never have lived. Although there are groups that assist with fund raising now, Maggie has spent long decades battling to keep the home running on meager funds.

Outside politics

Some women's organizations have deliberately tried to keep politics off their agendas, like the South African National Consumer Union, South African Co-ordinating Consumer Council and the Women's Bureau. Margaret Lessing, a pioneer woman journalist in London and then South Africa, has been a stalwart leader in all these organizations, and has often been honored for her contribution to women's and consumer issues over the decades.

Other women's organizations have been organized along cultural lines like the Suid Afrikaanse Vroue Federasie ("sayt AFri-kaan-sa FRo-wa FAY-DAY-ra-ssi") and the Federale Vroueraad Volksbeleging ("fay-da-RAA-lay FRo-wa-raat FOLKS-bay-lay-gging"), both aimed at Afrikaner women and their needs. These organizations are generally Calvinist and conservative in their philosophy, but believe totally in women's power. They spend a lot of energy campaigning against issues like drug abuse and other social ills.

The achievements of these and many other women's organizations and all the women who have given their loyal support may pass without much fanfare. But they have made a major impact on the individual lives of millions of their fellow South Africans.

Unity is strength Some organizations have been set up to join women of all races to work for a better country. The Federation of South African Women was formed in the mid-1950s to unite women to fight for their rights and to give them the confidence to make their own decisions. Many of FEDSAW's leaders were banned, imprisoned or fled into exile. However, the movement has seen a revival since the '80s as women became tired of the men's view that their place was only in the home.

In 1976 Women for Peace was co-founded by Bridget Oppenheimer, wife of one of the biggest business tycoons in the country, and Dr. Cecile Celliers, who felt they could not "sit around doing nothing" while the country was in crisis after the student uprisings. Compassion and dedication sum up this organization's commitment to peace through communication across the cultural divides.

Of a more political nature, the United Democratic Front Women's Congress was formed to coordinate national campaigns of existing women's organizations, and also to encourage new ones to be formed throughout the country in the '80s. The African National Congress re-formed its Women's League in 1991 after it had been banned 30 years before with the banning of the ANC. Some of the aims of this organization are to: formulate an ANC policy of women's liberation and the promotion of women's development; lead a national debate on a Charter of Women's Rights; and unite scores of women's organizations on a national level.

Trade unions

As we have seen, women were very active in the formation of the earliest trade unions. As they entered the work force in the '20s and '30s, so they marshalled support from their colleagues for improved conditions and a fair wage. Women's rights were also on their agenda. However, this first groundswell of enthusiasm was slowly battered by the waves of segregationist laws and slowly much of the unions' influence was curtailed, if only temporarily.

As large sectors of the population had no political rights, it was inevitable that the new union movement that burst into the '70s and '80s was a more militant and politically driven one. The divisions in the country were echoed in the unions. There were black and white unions, left- and right-wing unions, but the voice of women was always heard.

"Sellout or saint?" A stalwart, who weathered all storms, who lived to tell her tale despite harassment and imprisonment from the right, and fire-bombings of her home from the ultra-left, is Lucy Mvubelo ("mm-VU-bay-lo"). Despite the persecution, she stuck to her beliefs and principles, leading one of the biggest unions until her retirement in the mid-1980s.

Lucy started work in the clothing industry in 1941 as a machinist and within the space of a very few years had founded the National Union of Clothing Workers. As general secretary she held the union together when all of apartheid's laws separating different races within unions were breaking over her head. She believed quite firmly in a middle-of-the-road policy for the sake of the people, the workers.

For years she fought for the recognition of black unions with full privileges and rights. With this approach she knew the union could then improve the lot and pay of workers. Although called a government stooge by some left-wing unionists, she believed firmly in the route she had chosen.

"I felt that if I advocated boycotts I would be putting a spear into the back of my people," she says.

When black women first began working in jobs other than domestic work, it was in the garment and textile factories that they found employment. It is therefore not surprising that the first black woman to found a union, Lucy Mvubelo, was from the clothing industry.

Affirmative action Being very firmly in favor of multi-racialism, Lucy also fought tooth and nail for the freedom of unions to decide for themselves if they wished to be segregated or not and not have the government impose the divisions on them.

Lucy strongly opposed the withdrawal of investments by American and European businesses as she felt it would lead to more discrimination against black workers. As jobs became more scarce they would be given to whites, not blacks. The jobless urban blacks would then be forced into homelands, destitute and unproductive rural areas. In the '70s Lucy also advocated that foreign companies employ an affirmative action program for black school leavers, training them eventually for senior positions. Although at this time such action was against the law, foreign companies took heed of her persuasion.

The dilemma of whether Lucy Mvubelo was a "sellout" or a "saint," is a complex matter. In her own words, "I have done so much to better the lives of individual black South Africans." After 37 years of active commitment to her union, there are many who would agree. Whether women workers feel her middle-of-the-road stand was right or wrong, no one can deny how much Lucy Mvubelo did for women and workers in her valiant fight for union recognition.

The law: The long road ahead

While many modern democracies have legislated equality for women in the 20th century, South African women are still disadvantaged to some extent by both racism and sexism, rooted to a large extent in the legal system. In recent times, however, women are no longer prepared to accept this and are working through various organizations to change their situation.

Both the South African Law Commission and the Women's Legal Status Committee, which was formed in the mid-1970s, have focussed on crucial issues in the law that affect women. They included: education; child care; abortion; employment, where some 70 laws established lower minimum payment for women; enforced joint taxation for married women. The special problems of African women in connection with both tribal law and common law needed to be resolved.

Thanks to the continuous efforts of these organizations some laws have been scrapped, while others have been amended to give married women almost the same status as their husbands, allow separate taxation for married women and enforce certain maternity benefits and rights. The laws of divorce now allow women access to their husband's pension, and also give right of maintenance to either spouse, instead of only to women. A wife's contribution to the home and family is taken into account in a divorce settlement.

Although many laws have been changed to be fairer to women and children, it is an ongoing process. The fight is not over yet. Women still hope for further improvements in the law to enhance their quality of life in the fields of child care, divorce maintenance payments as well as a more enlightened approach to acts of abuse and violence against women. A children's rights charter has also been proposed.

Waiting their turns at the child care and family planning clinic. Child care is one area which the law can provide for, to improve the quality of life of women.

At the top Added to the voice of many hundreds of women magistrates, attorneys and barristers, is that of Justice Leonara van den Heever. She has reached the pinnacle of her profession, making a major impact on women and society at large.

Although Justice Leonora van den Heever grew up in the midst of the legal world—her father was a prominent judge—she at first studied to be a schoolteacher. She had been encouraged to enter the legal profession, but she felt she did not want to "walk in [her father's] shadow."

However, it was not long before she completed her law examinations and entered the profession. At times she worked from home to be near her three children.

A woman of great integrity and charming personality, Leonora took the silk, that is became a judge, in 1968. In doing so, she took the hopes of many women to the bench with her as she was known for her concern with women's and children's matters. Now South Africa's first-ever woman judge has been appointed to the Appellate Division of the Supreme Court, the highest court of law in the land. Justice Leonora van den Heever reached for the sky—and touched it.

Medicine: The doctor is a woman!

The nursing and related health care profession, despite the long, selfless hours and the low pay, has always been dominated by women. But today's South Africa also has a fairly high percentage of women making inroads into hospital administration and the medical field, and now even boasts a woman Minister for National Health and Population Development. Women's success in this field can perhaps be attributed, tongue-in-cheek, to the fact that one of the first surgeons at the Cape, Dr. James Barry, was found to be a woman only when she died!

Dr. Phyllis Knocker is the first woman surgeon ever to be admitted to the prestigious Fellowship of the Royal College of Surgeons in England.

It's a man's world Although she is a woman in a male domain, there is no mistaking ground-breaking Dr. Rina Venter for a man. As Minister for National Health and Population Development, she is South Africa's first-ever woman Cabinet Minister. In a nutshell, her portfolio means looking at the health of the country, says Rina, who has a doctorate in social work.

Realistically she has to deal with issues like AIDS, drug abuse, population control and the lack of adequate health care for certain sectors of society, like the mushrooming informal housing areas and the overcrowded, strife-torn townships. Her aim is to try and find as many solutions as possible. She is a bold woman who says "I will fight for any human cause," and means it, as she demonstrated when she opened the previously racially segregated hospitals to all races. She reasons simply, "There is an over-supply of white hospitals, and an under-supply of black hospitals. Thus the only moral thing to do is to open the hospitals to provide health care to all."

Community medicine Linking medicine and a strong sense of community

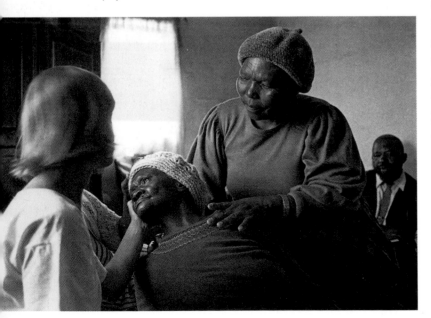

A doctor from a community health project attends to an elderly blind patient in a squatter township. Many women doctors volunteer their services in such projects.

concern is the forte of Dr. Khorshed Ginwala, specialist and lecturer in community medicine at one of the country's major universities. She has packed more into her 60 years than most people would achieve in many lifetimes, serving on a number of professional and community organizations.

Although she was born in Bombay, India, her parents returned to South Africa immediately after her birth. Khorshed later completed her high school education in India and studied medicine in Ireland. Then, in London, she received a certificate in hospital administration and completed a master's degree in community health before returning home. Having always felt great concern and sympathy for the underprivileged communities, she chose to study medicine as she felt it was one of the areas of greatest need in the country. She is a strong supporter of a national health system and believes that, while doctors should have the freedom to practice privately, they should also be obliged to do a certain amount of community health work.

Khorshed, who is a wife and mother of three sons, has been very active as the president of the Indian Child and Family Welfare Society (which is now non-racial) and was the deputy superintendent of a large hospital. She has received numerous awards for her work in the community, has presented numerous papers at conferences and has

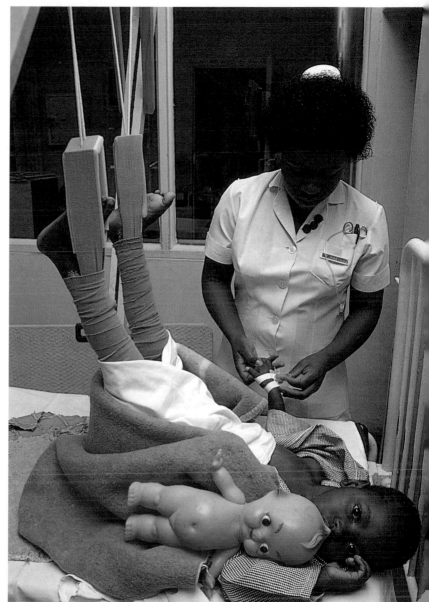

had many of her works published. Although soft-spoken and frail-looking, she has boundless energy, and has recently also become the chairperson of the branch of the African National Congress in her neighborhood.

Nursing is a traditionally accepted field of work for women.

Sangoma

A *sangoma*, or witchdoctor—an African medicine person—is chosen by the ancestral spirits to dedicate his or her life to the benefit of their people. Mainly women, *sangoma* are priests, prophets, physicians, herbalists, psychologists, diviners, rain-makers and exorcists all in one. A witchdoctor takes a holistic approach to medicine, attempting to cure not only the disease, but to treat the whole person, body and soul. Most often a *sangoma* only asks for payment if the treatment is successful.

The word "sangoma" means "one who is called to the profession," usually through dreams. Because the calling comes from the realms of the ancestral spirits, the chosen person has very little choice in the matter, and those that have resisted for a while have been known to become ill, either mentally or physically. The chosen person follows the messages in her dreams until she finds her teacher. She is then apprenticed and has to endure a long process of training which includes instruction in the spiritual realms and the use and preparation of herbal remedies. There is no set period of training, but it usually takes two or three years before a novice goes through the first initiation ceremony which allows her to practice. (Picture shows a young *sangoma* at her initiation ceremony.)

Witchdoctors claim the basis of their herbal knowledge comes to them from their ancestral spirits, who in turn learned it from the original Bushmen, or Khoisan, who were believed to be masters of this art. Herbs are usually gathered from the veld and almost every herb has a special song which is sung both when it is picked and when it is prepared. Usually herbs are ground, mixed in various proportions and then added to water, but some are powdered and used in the nose like snuff or smoldered on an ember and the smoke inhaled. Their uses are both medicinal and magical.

There are also pure herbalists (who are not *sangoma*) who supply herbal remedies in much the same way as a Western pharmacist supplies medicines.

The media: A media mogul in the making

As in most parts of the world, women in South Africa make up more than 50% of the media industry, although very few women have battered the male bastions of newspaper editorship and management. Making a striking exception to this norm is owner, manager, and editor-in-chief Jane Raphaely.

Born and educated in the United Kingdom, Jane moved to South Africa where she joined a public relations company and was told that although she could write, she would never make a journalist. How far wrong was the person who said this.

Reaching new heights As founder and editor for nearly 20 years of the largest circulation English-language women's magazine in the country, Jane certainly made her mark on journalism. As if to make a point, she then clinched a deal with the highly successful American *Cosmopolitan* magazine to publish it in South Africa.

With her previous employer, a major magazine publisher, putting up half the capital, Jane Raphaely Associates became a 50% owner of a new publishing empire. Despite local skepticism because of the magazine's avant garde and very modern approach, Jane's business turned a profit in only 18 months—a world record for any magazine from the Hearst empire, the American owners of *Cosmopolitan*.

For her efforts Jane was voted Business Woman of the Year. As if spurred by this latest accolade, she promptly bought a local women's magazine which she has improved both in content and circulation. A good journalist cannot be kept down.

Jane Raphaely, a media mogul against many odds.

Business: The toughest barriers

Attitudes toward women in business are slowly changing, but South Africa still lags far behind the rest of the industrialized world in realizing women are an essential part of the work force. Even though sexual discrimination was outlawed in 1988, sexist job reservation is still very much in practice. Perhaps women are in some ways to blame for not challenging their employers.

Although some companies may outwardly agree to equal opportunities and even affirmative action plans, most have very few, if any, women at board level. It still holds true that a woman has to be better to compete with her male peers. This is a sad state of affairs, as it is felt that if businesses did use women effectively, the country's severe managerial shortage could be overcome.

The official statistics for the economically active work force in South Africa is about 11 million. Over 7 million workers are men and more than 3.6 million are women. However, this is not a totally accurate reflection of the work force as there are many people involved in the informal sector as hawkers, part-time domestic workers, baby-sitters in the community and the like. A large proportion of these informal workers are women.

More than 40 years ago the Johannesburg Business and Professional Women's Club was founded, and to this day businesswomen feel the need for its continued existence as "they are playing in a predominantly male field." A Business Woman of the Year award is used to encourage women achievers as well as to give status and recognition to their achievements. Despite men seeming to dominate the business world, a number of women have fought their way to the top, most often running their own companies.

The unfair odds The dice is loaded against black women even more as they have to contend with cultural discrimination from their own community and racial discrimination from other communities. However, statistics show that the few women that are in senior positions are the top black earners, above their menfolk.

Susan Molete, management accountant of a bank with her sights set on the top spot, is one of them. She says if women could all believe in what they do and not think of how many heads would roll if they did it, they would break all the barriers that stand in their way. It is they, and nobody else, who will change how society views women.

Sweet success Marina Maponya, Soweto's most famous millionaire, seems to have taken this view without even thinking about it. Having completed a social work diploma, she married a Soweto businessman who owned a small dairy. In the mid-1950s her husband became so involved in the Johannesburg African Chamber of Commerce that Marina took over the running of the dairy. It is hard to believe that a day that started at 4 a.m., supervising the filling of milk bottles, was the beginning of her highly-successful business career.

The business consisted of 20 deliverymen on bicycles, but within four years it had grown to 100 deliverymen, and annual turnover had increased from $33,000 to $270,000. Marina saw the gap and soon opened a butchery in Soweto for the fast-expanding population. In three years the turnover had increased from $60,000 to almost $1 million. The dairy, under a manager, was not the success it should be, so she sold it. She used the money to build a one-stop shopping center with a general store, a restaurant and a fruit and vegetable store, adjacent to her butchery.

In the mid-1970s the Maponyas floated a number of their companies, that is sold shares to the public, sold a number of other shops they owned and used the money to start a garage business, also in Soweto. To make this venture a success, Marina found it needed her dedication to hard work and her knowledge of sensible risk taking.

So she employed a manager for the shopping center, and took over as managing director of the garage, an area of business so often considered men's territory. Two years later she got the dealership of one of South Africa's biggest car manufacturers, and it is now the largest service station in the southern hemisphere with an annual turnover of millions of dollars. Marina has a 50% share in the business and is also involved in a construction company, a funeral parlor and a marketing business, among others.

Business Woman of the Year Marina Maponya. Her attitude to life has not changed with her increased fortune. She finds time to be involved with the Black Housewives' League, the Cripple Care Association and the Women's Missionary Society.

African singer. It is in the liberal field of the arts that women find full expression.

The world of showbiz

For many centuries South Africa has been a melting pot of cultures and this has led to an entertainment world as diverse as the people who take part in it. Women have found a freedom in this more liberal field, unrestrained by political or sexist bias. The tumultuous political situation has also stimulated a raw creativity, allowing women's talents full rein, often at an international level, in art, literature, music, theater and dance.

A delicate art

Women artists hold their own today, winning awards and selling their work to collectors and museums throughout the country and on the international market. Their diversity is large.

The unassuming and rather shy Cythna Letty was one of the world's leading botanical illustrators, receiving great acclaim and international awards for her work in over 60 scientific publications as well as in many exhibitions. As a young child she learned to love the flowers of the veld, and although she had no formal training in art, her innate skill, self study and determination made her a world master of her discipline.

A tribute to rural roots Along with many other South African women, Helen

Sibidi's work is now sought after internationally. Although she started out as a domestic worker, she came from a rural family of traditional artists—both her great-grandmother and her grandmother were potters. She has always remained very involved with her family and says her work and home life are very intertwined. Helen's work in watercolors, charcoals and oils has won her awards at home and abroad, but she says, "I'm not a proud person. My way is traditional, the way my grandmother taught me. It is not for me to accept the praise." Her road to becoming an artist has been full of dust and stones, poverty and hope. But Helen is also a beacon, a representative, for all the thousands of anonymous rural women whose art extends from intricate and colorful murals to decorated pots, beadwork and finely-woven basketwork.

If music be the food of love...

In traditional African society music was not merely a form of entertainment or an expression of creativity. It was linked totally with life and the community. Making music was a social event, and was seen as a necessity, not a luxury.

Women's voices as diverse as opera diva Mimi Coertse ("COORT-sa") and Miriam Zenzile ("ZEN-zee-lay") Makeba have reached out to the rest of the world and drawn great acclaim. So great was the voice of the young Mimi Coertse that after only three years of training in Vienna, Austria, she was quickly signed up by the famous Vienna State Opera. There she sang leading roles in all the famous operas before the world's most discerning audiences for 19 years. From when she was a very little girl, Mimi knew she would be an opera singer. "I had such drive, I had a demon in me," she says of her early days. Mimi is still very involved in the opera, both as a diva and in encouraging new young singers.

Miriam Zenzile Makeba (profiled in Chapter 5) found international stardom, singing out against apartheid. She is world famous for her "click-song," where she uses her traditional African language to create an effect that is almost instrumental in sound.

Helen Sibidi, artist. She began as a domestic worker, but happily her talent was discovered and she is now an internationally-known artist.

The call of the stage

The earliest African societies had rich and varied dramatic forms. The Khoikhoi and Khoisan loved mime, dance and music, using costumes and makeup to great effect, while the Nguni were famous for dramatic narratives. In 1607 the first Shakespeare play was

The Isetazini Theater. With a wealth of cultural heritage, the South African theater scene is very rich. Women are not only involved on stage, but backstage as well, as writers, producers and directors.

acted by seamen on a vessel at anchor in Cape Town. As the different cultures changed and urbanized, so theater took on a more Western style.

Janice Honeyman, famous as an actress, director and TV presenter, sums up South African theater when she says, "It's a very rich theatrical scene in South Africa—everything from African versions of the classics and political satire to traditional British-type comedy and farce. In a way we would be theatrically poorer if the situation were

better here…but change is what we are working for." Janice, who has written and adapted many plays and recently also directed opera, was asked to direct a Shakespeare production for the Royal Shakespeare Company in London. She received high praise for this.

Born to act Equally versatile and famous actress Nomsa Nene ("NOM-sa nay-nay") acted in the townships until she joined Johannesburg's experimental theater group. A brilliant actress, she took the famous play, *Poppie*, to the rest of the world, making a great hit in New York. She has won almost every theatrical award in the country and has acted in roles as different as Shakespeare and the classics and contemporary protest theater.

Nomsa believes she was born to act. She says it is where she belongs. "I don't belong anywhere else. I'm dedicated to my art with all my heart. There is no way I can ever neglect it." It is with the same strength that she addresses women's issues, saying, "If you know what you want you can get it….it's no good just saying to yourself, you're a woman and then giving up."

It has not always been an easy road for Nomsa, who worked as a sales assistant in a clothing store when she was trying to make her way as an actress. And, much like in the theater, she used her bubbly personality to break down barriers among her colleagues and her clients. But there is a seriousness beneath all her laughter as she says women must work together to solve their problems. "If we start caring more, so many things could change. I've always walked proudly down the street. I've always believed this is my country too."

The world of words

The poignant issues women are confronted with almost on a daily basis have pushed women writers to great heights, as is borne out by Nadine Gordimer's Nobel Prize for Literature, awarded in 1991. (She is profiled in Chapter 5.) Women have been prolific writers through the decades, and Olive Schreiner was one of the first feminist writers in the country. She wrote her most poignant work, *The Story of an African Farm*, in 1883. This novel condemns women's subordinate status in society and caused a great deal of consternation all over the world at the time.

Stirring the nation's conscience In more recent times a book written by one woman about the life of another woman caused a major stir at home and in many foreign countries too. Elsa Joubert, an Afrikaner journalist turned poet and author, wrote a novel based on the factual account of the hardships faced by a Xhosa woman as she tried to find employment amid the tangle of apartheid laws.

Anjte Krog, poet.

This book is more than an exposé of the hardships caused by apartheid. It describes the hopes and fears and, most of all, the struggle of a woman trying to bring up her family on her own. *The Long Journey of Poppie Nongena*, as it is called, has been translated into many foreign languages, and adapted as a play that received great praise at home and in New York. It has won a number of literary awards, including one for the English translation, done by Elsa. The film rights are also being discussed. As a gesture of solidarity of one woman with another, this courageous writer has donated half of all her royalties to "Poppie," making her struggle all but over.

> **Shirley Mphuti dared to enter the all-male territory of soccer. Recently she refereed a competitive soccer match at high school level. Definitely a first.**

Sport: Whose turf is this anyway?

Living in a warm, sunny country, South Africans place a lot of emphasis on recreational sports and outdoor activities, but men tended to be the participants while women stood on the sideline and watched. However, attitudes are changing slowly, and in the last decade or two women have become more active and competitive.

Despite early resistance, there have been women who have held their own in international sports, although the sports boycott of South Africa by international sports bodies, which has just been lifted, dampened enthusiasm a bit. As a 12-year-old, Karen Muir was South Africa's greatest swimmer, and by the time she had turned 16 she had 15 world records to her name. Today she is a medical doctor, but her fame lives on as she has been given a special place in America's International Hall of Fame—the first South African to be honored in this way.

Ilana Kloss played cricket for her junior school, and had she been a boy, she would probably have gone on to play it at an international level. Instead she settled for tennis and won the Wimbledon Junior title in 1972. She then successfully entered the ranks of professional tennis and today works in a major American professional tennis organization.

At school both boys and girls are encouraged to do sport, but in some communities there is still a feeling that girls and women "should play a more subservient role in the home." Unfortunately this means that there are very few black women runners alongside the country's world-class male athletes. There are a number of white women runners of world class—Charmaine Gayle, Sonya Laxton, Frith van der Merwe, and Zola Budd, probably the most famous of all.

The uneven load

South Africa's women have achieved a great deal. Some have headed for direct competition with their male peers, some have turned in a conflict and many have just got out there and done what needed to be done. Rarely are they encouraged by their men, their families, their communities. Very rarely do they get any hands-on help from their husbands who to a large extent have not yet moved to take up their share of household responsibilities, which they still regard as women's work!

Galloping gold mine

Zola Budd's career is fairly typical of women athletes, as even she has at times put her home and family life ahead of her running career, and her conservative rural background was of little help in coping with the pressures of international athletics. In 1991 she made her comeback at the same stadium where, in 1984, as a barefoot 17-year-old, she broke the world 5,000 meters record by clipping an incredible 6.43 seconds off it. (Her time was 15 minutes 1.83 seconds.)

Her incredible speed catapulted her from hometown applause to cold, wet England where the crowds resented her. And where, she felt, everyone from the press to the advertisers to the coaches saw her as a money-making machine, a galloping gold mine. Four years later, even though she had broken many records, she returned home with a foot injury and close to a nervous breakdown from the stress of international pressures. She stopped running and turned her back on the world. Well almost. She met and married a businessman.

Today Zola says marriage has brought a balance and stability into her life, and although studying computer programing, she has begun to run again. This time she is running competitively for the sheer pleasure of it.

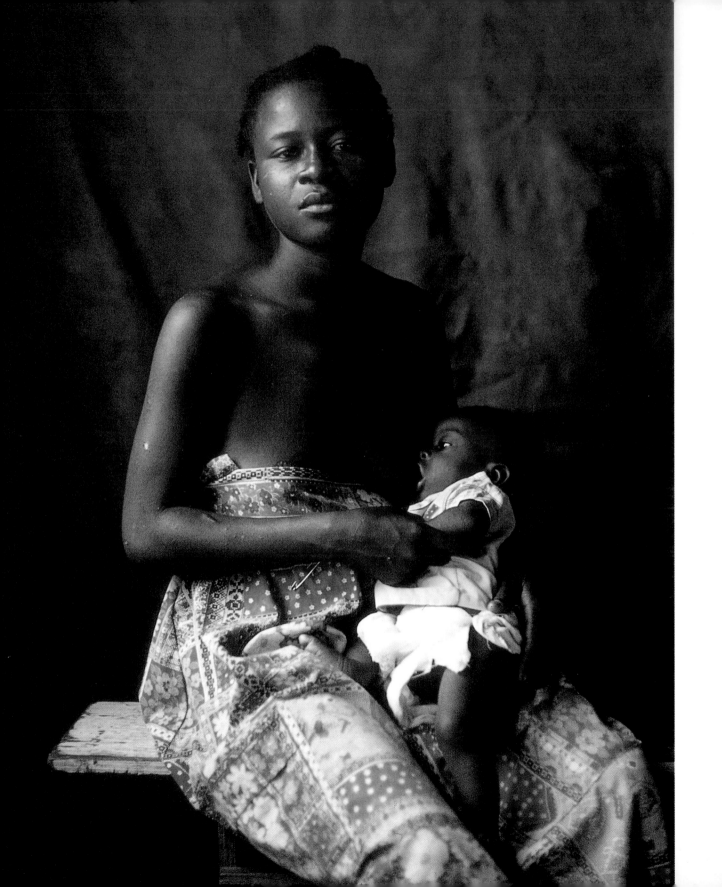

chapter four

Being Woman

ociety in South Africa has so many divisions, both by race and by economic well-being, and the status of women is different in each group. But there is one common factor: Women in any group are less than equal to men. Although in recent times some laws have been amended to allow women more equality with men, the reality lags far behind. Also, feminism and women's liberation have not yet become major factors in the country as they have in America and Europe because political issues have taken precedence.

Being woman, an African woman

In the African society, by far the largest in the country, there is a lack of concern, especially by men, about women's desires and needs. There is also a lack of appreciation of the role women play in holding together the family unit. This is mainly because there has been a watering down of rural traditions in the African society's transition to urban life and a Western value system. Many of the rural traditions played a very important role of checks and balances in a tribal hierarchy. A woman's life may not always have been easy, but her role was as clearly defined as her husband's. In most cases the censure, or disapproval, of the extended family or even the whole clan or section of the tribe would be used to ensure she was treated with the dignity and respect she deserved.

Opposite: Women's work—bringing up children is considered the responsibility of a woman, and men will do little to help in this area.

Right: Pottery—women of Africa have refined pot-making to an art.

Price of industrialization Africans, and especially the women, have been most affected by the country's rapid industrialization. Their own social order was broken in the urbanization process. It now no longer works as a complete and distinct entity. The basic parts of these traditional cultures—like the subsistence economy, joint and extended families, an elaborate network of family ties, the *lobola* or bride-price (described in Chapter 6), devotion to ancestors and hereditary chieftainship—have withered away or blended with urban, Western values. Often women are caught in the vacuum this has caused: they are not protected in the way of the old tribal culture nor by the civil law.

The legal system in South Africa is based on a Western system, but it does make allowances for African customary law which, especially in cases referring to marital status and women, is very different from Western norms. Although customary law reflects the old, traditional society, it has been poorly adapted to the changes in the social conditions and human relations brought about by industrialization and urbanization. Women now tend to be worse off in terms of customary law than before industrialization. The main reason for this is that women have outgrown the status given to them in a traditional society. It is also felt that the male-dominated courts have at times interpreted the law to the disadvantage of women.

An example of how a woman's status can be affected by either the tribal or customary law, or the civil or Western style law, is clearly shown in the laws affecting marriage. Any woman can get married by civil law, and these laws have recently been changed to give women equal status with men in the marriage. African women can also marry by customary law, and quite a large number, especially in the rural areas, do this in keeping with their cultural heritage. However, customary laws can disadvantage women for they limit women's right to own property and allow polygamy.

African women in the cities As ever larger numbers of rural women move to towns and cities in search of work, so the pattern of life is changing from an extended family to a nuclear family, or single person or parent. There is also a change in the way women look at marriage and what it has to offer. Their attitudes depend a lot on whether they are young or old, traditional or Christian, educated or uneducated. Men and women also tend to disagree on the changing roles of women.

In South African society, and especially in the black communities, service work is seen as women's work,

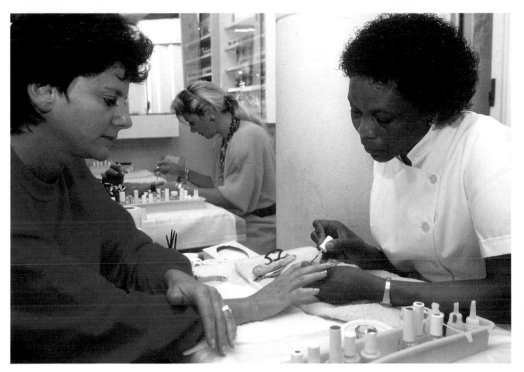

A manicurist at work. Service jobs are generally filled by African women.

and this extends to the home where women are always expected to serve and care for the families. Few men—from any cultural group—will help with this work. Women are expected to see to it that everybody in the family gets food. Men may often demand a meal even if there is very little or no money available, even when they have not contributed any money to the running of the home. Mothers are also expected to see that children are provided with clothes. Sometimes women have to borrow money to make ends meet.

This has led to many types of voluntary organizations being formed to help women cope with the pressures of urban life, the most important being those that help with household savings. They are usually called *stokvels* ("stock-fells") or *mohodisano* ("MOE-dis-sa-no") which means "we pay each other back." Each group has about 30 members and they all pool a sum of money each month with one person taking all the money once in rotation. This allows the family to have a lump sum of cash to buy in bulk or to purchase larger consumer goods without having to buy on time, which is costly, or take out a loan. The meetings, held at a different member's home each time, are also social occasions where food and drinks may be served and problems can be discussed. Great emphasis is placed on moral and social support.

The move to the cities Although tough laws of the past tried to prevent women from living and working in the urban areas, the poverty and lack of employment in the rural areas forced many to break the law and seek work, any work, in the cities. With the political changes in the country at present, these laws have been scrapped.

African women work in almost every profession in the country, but the numbers in relation to the size of their group—Africans make up some 70% of the population—are very low indeed. However, they are increasing as women's education, attitudes and opportunities change. The nursing and teaching professions employ the highest number of women as they have been "open" to women for many decades. Although these professions are essential to the community, they lack the status and high salaries of other professions.

In strange contrast, the few African women who are in very senior positions in companies and corporations in the major cities are generally in one of the higher income groups in the country, according to a recent survey.

Most women HAVE to work African women today mainly work as farm laborers, while in the urban areas domestic work is their main source of employment. These women work because they need to—their income is essential to the well-being of their families. An increasing number also work in the service industry and in factories.

This was not always so. Over 100 years ago most African women lived in rural areas with their men and families. They plowed the land, grew crops, cooked, cared for the children and made the utensils they needed in their homes. Once gold was discovered in 1886, the migrant labor system was developed where the men went to work on the mines for long periods, often as long as a year without returning home.

The women and children, and the very old men who could no longer work, remained in the rural areas. This meant women mainly had to do the heavy work of the men so as to try and live off the land. In many instances this breaking down of the family unit led to abject poverty and misery. Women were supposed to get special permission if they wanted to join their husbands in town.

> **South Africa's population of some 35 million people is made up of the following groups:**
> • 70.2% Africans
> • 16.3% whites
> • 10.4% Coloreds
> • 3.1% Asians

In the '20s only about six out of every 100 women lived in towns as jobs were few and men did a lot of the domestic work for affluent families. But as industries grew, men found employment in these areas, and women took on the role of domestic worker.

Home away from home Today there are at least 2 million domestic workers in South Africa, mainly employed by affluent whites, although more and more middle-class black families have house help as well. They usually live in, that is live with the family they work for, or work as part-timers, working a day or two each week for two or three employers. In rural areas domestic workers are employed in farm homesteads too.

Although they are slowly unionizing under the South African Domestic Workers' Union, domestic workers are still among the worst paid and least protected employees in South Africa. Unfair dismissal, very long working hours, very little or no annual leave are some of their major grievances.

Until recently laws forbade live-in workers from having their husbands or children living with them if they were living with white families. This often led to the situation where women would be looking after their employers' children while their own children were cared for by grandparents in the

townships or homelands. These children would see their mothers perhaps only once or twice a year.

Domestic work fits the description of "women's work" in every way as employees spend their days, and often nights too, serving others. Most often their work is the same as what they do at home for their own families—cooking, cleaning the house, doing the washing and ironing and taking care of the children. The view many South Africans, especially men, have of women's role in society, is affected by the fact that the highest number of women in employment are domestic workers.

After the day's work is done, the domestic worker returns to her little room where, alone, she thinks of her family and children, perhaps hundreds of miles away.

A boom in service jobs Women also work at semi- and unskilled jobs in the factories. With the economic boom in the '70s many more service jobs like office cleaning, hairdressing, waitressing and tea-making, clerical and sales work became available, and some women were able to move out of domestic work into these jobs.

Today growing numbers of black women are heads of households. That is, they are the main breadwinners for the family. There are a number of reasons for this: the urban divorce rate is increasing, and in the rural areas large numbers of men are migrant workers who may stop sending money home, so the women have to go out and work.

Many married women have to work as their men may be unemployed or earn wages too low to support the family.

Also, the number of African women professionals has trebled in the last 20 years, while the increase in the numbers in management and administration has jumped hundreds of percent. But the price is high as many husbands cannot cope with the cultural change of the woman's role, leading to a very high divorce rate. In some areas of urban South Africa, over 57% of African households are headed by women.

The role of rural women The most common work rural women are able to find is either on white-owned farms or

A day in the life of an urban worker

Dora Mhlangu ("mm-SHLANG-gu") no longer has a husband. She was married once, by tribal law, but as there is no documentary proof of this, and she cannot find him in the huge sprawling township of Soweto, she cannot even get maintenance for their two children. She now has a boyfriend who is the father of her baby.

She rises at about 4:30 in the morning to prepare breakfast for her two school-age children. On the way to the busstop, she must drop her youngest at a baby-sitter's home and then catch the 5:30 bus to the city. In the townships roads are inadequate and transportation poor and congested. Once in the city of Johannesburg, she catches a second bus out to the neighborhood where she works as a domestic worker. She tries to reach her employer's home by about 7:30 a.m. Her chores there include cleaning the house, doing the washing and ironing, and helping to take care of her employer's children. She tries to leave at about four in the afternoon to get home before dark, but often only reaches home well after 5:30.

Once she steps into her home, her "second shift" begins immediately. She must cook the evening meal, clean, wash and iron her family's clothes, and take care of her children, who have had no supervision since leaving school at midday. She leaves the heavier work, knitting, sewing and mending, for weekends. Dora has very little, if any, time for herself, but usually manages to attend a Sunday morning church service.

African women in the rural areas work as farm laborers on white-owned farms, or they farm their own land.

in the "border" industries that have been set up on the edge of the homelands, rural areas where most African people were supposed to live. Most of these jobs involve heavy manual labor and are badly paid as there are many more unemployed people than there are jobs.

Women who are employed in the border industry factories are rarely protected by the trade unions as they fear they could face dismissal if they become involved in union activities—there are thousands waiting to take their place even with the low salaries and bad working conditions.

Tilling the land One in three African women is an agricultural worker, either farming her own land in the homelands or working on white-owned farms for very low wages. Often they are forced into these jobs due to rural poverty. Many women farm workers are migrants, employed on a daily or seasonal basis during the picking and harvesting times. They are paid very low wages and sometimes paid only in kind. For example, they are given produce as payment and then have to go and sell it to earn money. Others live on the farms and are employed as domestic or casual labor. Women are gradually taking over jobs men used to do, like working in dairies, on chicken farms and driving tractors, as they are often preferred by the farmers who find them more reliable and conscientious than men.

The triple burden No matter where women live and work they are primarily responsible for the family's health, wealth, and happiness. African women, as well as Colored and Asian women, tend to have a triple burden—they are discriminated against on the grounds of sex and race, and are also economically worse off. In the early '70s the government proposed minimum wage levels for unskilled workers, but allowed women to be paid less than men. In recent years new laws demand equal pay in theory, but are not always put into practice.

These three kinds of discrimination tend to reinforce each other and reforms in law—some have already been enacted—are not necessarily going to free women from this burden unless there are also other changes. There should be change in the tribal social relations, taking into account modern-day lifestyles, and there should be more educational opportunities. Affirmative action should be taken to increase the number of women in properly paid jobs. And women should participate in the various levels of government.

Being woman, a white woman

White women have been the most advantaged of all race groups, but as women, they are a long way from being equal to their men who have run the government, commerce and industry, the farms and the church.

A life in the country In the early part of this century rural white women were mainly farmers' wives. As they lived miles from towns or villages, their homestead became the center of the farm community.

They developed a degree of social responsibility—they were involved in most happenings on the farm, knew about and contributed to their husband's work and assisted their laborers when they or their children were ill or injured. The entire farm community would turn to the farmer's wife in times of need.

Farmers' wives had to develop a degree of self-sufficiency, growing much of their own food, making soap, bread, salted and preserved meats, and canned fruits and vegetables for winter. In more recent times the steady growth of towns and villages means most farmsteads are within an hour or two's drive from a supermarket or provision store. Most homes also have modern conveniences like refrigerators and freezers.

Because the children learned most of their moral tone from home—not being exposed to modern influences as they were in the cities—these white and

> **Wife and servant are the same, but only differ in the name.**
> —*Lady Chudleigh*

mainly Afrikaner communities remained very isolated and conservative, even as they are today. Women still play second fiddle to their men, especially in politics, and are often submissive homemakers.

English-speaking men usually received professional training, had a craft or went into administration or business, while Afrikaner men were mainly farmers or miners. This meant Afrikaner women were more restricted in their employment opportunities than their English-speaking sisters. The attitude of the Dutch Reformed Church to women made Afrikaner women sub-servient to men. Because of their lack of education and isolated lives in the rural areas, Afrikaner women needing to work became factory workers. When factories were encouraged to move to the edge of African homelands, working-class Afrikaner women were badly affected.

Many Afrikaners have become urbanized, but even in these communities women usually work to help support the family and rarely see their work in terms of a career. Of course there have always been exceptions, and today many more of the younger generation are determined career women.

Afrikaner women in the countryside live an isolated life and are usually subservient to their men.

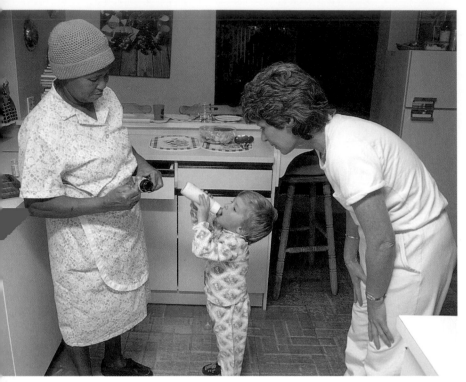

children and another to cook and clean. Their homes are large and luxurious, with well-kept gardens, swimming pools and, in the most affluent areas, even a tennis court.

For those who do not work, life often becomes a merry-go-round of bridge (a card game) parties, coffee mornings, book clubs and other social engagements. Children are encouraged to do a lot of activities after school, like swimming, music or ballet lessons, and mothers become the children's taxi drivers. Partly, this is caused by the lack of adequate public transportation throughout the country.

There is also an increasing number of career women who are constantly trying to juggle work, running a home and caring for their children. Although this puts a lot of strain on them—most South African men help very little in domestic issues—they are not as badly off as their Western sisters as they do have more home help. However, businesses and companies are not yet in tune with the needs of working mothers.

Women in the urban areas, whether working or not, usually have a domestic worker to help keep house and care for the children.

A more affluent approach The English-speaking white community has always been mainly urban and is generally seen to be more liberal both politically and socially. It is generally affluent and influenced by international trends. A high percentage of these women are well educated, usually to college level. But once they start a family, many leave their jobs and rarely return.

Married white women in urban areas who are raising families, whether or not they are working, usually employ full-time domestic workers or chars (part-time domestic worker). Some may even have one person to look after the

Not everyone lives in splendor Life for the non-professional, or poorer white woman, is not so easy—even the wage of a secretary is barely enough to live on in an urban area. Poorer white families live in the densely populated high-rise apartment neighborhoods. Children have little activity outside of school and often have to take care of themselves while their mothers are at work. Some of these families still manage to employ a domestic worker to help care for the children.

Being woman, a Colored woman, an Asian woman

Colored and Asian women have experienced much of the same oppression as African women. They were also subjected to racial discrimination in jobs and education, to resettlement against their will, and to restrictions on where they could live and work. However, they are mostly urban people and have had better access to jobs and education. As smaller groups, they have also been able to be more supportive of each other and generally maintain a higher standard of living.

India, a cultural heritage The Indian community is made up of both Hindus and Moslems who, to a large extent, maintain their cultural identity and still keep close links with their mother country, India. Although some Indian women have been in the forefront of politics, academia, business and other professional fields, the majority still cling to their cultural roots. They remain in the background as wives and mothers,

Vocational training for deaf Indian girls— learning to sew.

and when the need arises as it often does, as semi-skilled and skilled workers.

Until only a few decades ago, the Indian community strongly resisted women going out to work. Girls had to stop going to school once they reached puberty, and some girls were not ever sent to school. As late as 1972, only 42% of secondary school children were girls, and even now, if there is a shortage of money, it is the girl's education that will be sacrificed. These figures are improving steadily and now, especially in Natal where most Indians live, a fair number of Indian girls receive higher education and have successful careers in the professions. The number of emancipated Indian women is increasing.

A community on its own A majority of the Colored community, coming from a similar background to the Afrikaners, has middle class aspirations and a traditional Calvinistic value system of male dominance. Women are almost entirely responsible for keeping house and caring for the family. Having been excluded from the processes of government for many years, this community has struggled to keep abreast with Western development. Much of the community is working class, and many of the women have found employment as domestic workers. They also entered the garment industry early this century, and have continued to play an important role ever since.

There is also a strong and growing Colored Moslem community which traces its roots some 300 years back to the Malaysian Moslems from Southeast Asia. In this group, women generally keep the Moslem faith, in which they are accorded great respect. But their role is confined within the family and home, and they are excluded from community decision making or any political role. Although traditional dress has mainly given way to modern Western clothes, many Moslem women are still modest, covering their heads with a scarf, and wearing trousers and long-sleeved blouses.

Children in the Alexandra township. Many children in the townships are left on their own during the day as their parents are at work and child care facilities are sorely lacking.

Child care

Twenty years ago most South African working women were single. Today 49% of working women are mothers. The largest group of women to enter the work force in the past 25 years has been women with children under the age of six.

Child care is the major problem of all working women as very little support is offered by the government. Business and industry have also been slow to see to the needs of mothers.

Thus, mothers are helping each other by forming playgroups, becoming baby-sitters, and setting up after-school care centers where homework is supervised and which give extra activities like swimming or ballet lessons. Increasingly schools are offering after-class care too.

Conditions for black working mothers are especially bad as there are not enough day care centers in the townships—for example, Soweto day care centers can only take in 6 out of every 100 children in need of day-time care. This has led to the development of a child care system. Older women, who are no longer working, will take care of a number of preschool children each day while their mothers are at work. This system is not always ideal as the older women sometimes do not have the energy to take care of a number of small children for long hours. It is also costly, especially for working-class women who do not earn good salaries.

From very early in South African history women have formed organizations and groups to rally support for a cause, to defend an ideal or simply as a means to get to know and support each other. Groups have been formed by young and old, feminists and conservatives, but they have been less effective than their counterparts in other countries. Perhaps the reason is in the policies of the country, which divide the people. In a new country under a new government, women will now be able to unite to form a strong force.

The collective power of women

South African women have a history of taking part in working class struggles. This dates back to their involvement in the Industrial and Commercial Workers Union and the Women Workers General Union of the '20s, and to the garment and textiles unions of the '30s. Thousands of white and Colored women went out on strike to try and stop wage cuts during the Depression in the '30s, and also to demand better working conditions.

As more African women joined the labor force, they became involved in the unions too. By the late '60s women formed a major part of the work force in textile, garment and shoe factories— work that came to be seen as "women's work." It was not surprising then that the National Union of Clothing Workers became the biggest black union at the time.

In the late '70s women again took full part in union protests, which began mainly because of the very low wages in times of very high inflation. Other issues included poor working conditions.

More recently women have been less active in union activities. One of the reasons is the "double shift" (that is, working at a job and taking care of the family and home) takes up almost all their time. Many women are unskilled, and in times of high unemployment they fear that they may be fired if they are too active in the union. Many women who are union members do not feel capable of becoming leaders. Also, women are often not respected by men and therefore are not voted into leadership positions.

There are some exceptions to this—women leaders who are at the forefront of the union movement. These leaders are beginning to ask for benefits for women workers, like maternity benefits and child care. In the years to come, women are expected to be the biggest force in the trade unions, where they will use their power to change the workplace to their and their family's advantage.

Women's economic contribution is essential

It is now recognized that the South African economy could not operate without the contribution of women. But women still face inequality in their careers and in work conditions. Today the sheer numbers of women in the work force—40%—have forced at least some changes in conditions in the workplace. Often, however, it is only in the more senior positions or in companies employing more white collar workers that conditions for women have improved. By and large the working class woman has much less cooperation from her employer, and her workplace is less woman-friendly. Less attention is paid to her needs, born of all the other demands made on her by her family and home life. Because of this, an increasing number of women have left their jobs and are running their own businesses. They can give themselves a more flexible work schedule or work from their home. Their success rate is very high—better than their male counterparts.

President of the South African Domestic Workers Union addressing union members. Women in the forefront of the union movement are asking for benefits for working women.

Money clout

With more and more women entering the work force, they are gaining an economic independence and a growing economic power. They wield power as consumers as they have never before, forcing major supermarket chains, banks and other retailers to take notice of women's needs.

Nearly half of all private investments on the Johannesburg stock exchange are owned by women and more than 40% of all checking and credit accounts with banks are held by women. Growing numbers of women are buying property, especially in Soweto where some 40% of the houses sold in the last few years were bought by women. Women are also buying bigger items like cars and major household appliances.

From a man's perspective

As in many other countries, South African women are not expected to need to work for personal fulfillment, to need to support themselves and their families, to want to have a profession or to make decisions about their own lives. In the white community this male chauvinist approach comes mainly from the Calvinist tradition and doctrines developed by the Afrikaners from as far back as Voortrekker times. The English-speaking community is not much more liberated than their Afrikaner brothers, as the feminist movements which swept the West, forcing changes in legislation and attitude, did not really take off in South Africa. The African man is no less chauvinist, using his traditional culture as basis for an outdated view of women as less than equal, even in industrialized and urbanized communities. He ignores the fact that in most households women are joint contributors to the family income, if not the sole breadwinner.

Looking ahead

In South Africa, as in most countries, women hold a broad spectrum of values. They range from the most determined feminists and career women to those who work to support their families, and those who do not work outside the home at all, having actively chosen to be homemakers and mothers. The past political turmoil has slowed the progress of women's freedom by slowing the progress of the whole nation. More often women chose to fight alongside their men for civil rights, rather than on their own for sexual equality and social status.

But now that political change is in process, women will have to look at a whole range of issues affecting their lives in the future South Africa. They include equal pay; discrimination in hiring, promotion and firing; the allocation of jobs based on gender; maternity and paternity leave; child care; flexible hours; and sexual harassment.

Perhaps women's freedom and political freedom can go hand in hand in the new South Africa. But whatever role she chooses, today's South African woman has an identity, a sense of self-worth and the knowledge that she is making a contribution.

The breadwinner syndrome

The breadwinner syndrome, or the way companies, corporations and the civil service determines who is the major provider of income in a family, is the cause of a lot of discrimination against women in the work force. It determines attitudes toward women's benefits like pension, housing subsidies, and medical aid.

A woman is most often excluded from a housing subsidy if she is married, regardless of whether her husband qualifies for one or not. She receives a smaller amount of pension than her male counterpart, and most often may not include her children or husband on her medical aid scheme. These decisions are based on the outdated idea that a man is the breadwinner in a household and ignore the fact that today there are a great many two-salary homes and single-parent families.

chapter five

Profiles of Women

T here have always been South African women prepared to stand up and be counted, women who have gone beyond the call of duty in their contribution to their country and the future of their people. The six famous women profiled in this chapter have in their own expressive ways worked for the improvement of society. Their tireless pursuit of their chosen goals and their indomitable spirits have made an indelible mark on the face of the nation. They will always be beacons for the future generations to follow.

Nadine Gordimer

Nadine Gordimer began to write at the age of nine or 10. "I did not know how my poem or story came out of myself," she once wrote. "It was directed at no one, was read by no one." She did not dream in those early years that this "most solitary and deeply marvelous of secrets—the urge to make with words— would become a vocation…" Even less so did she dream that it would one day put her among the ranks of the world's greatest authors as one of only seven women ever to win a Nobel Prize for Literature.

Opposite: Women today aspire to be more than somebody's daughter, wife, mother or daughter-in-law.

Right: Some of Nadine Gordimer's novels.

Humanitarian ideals awakened Born in 1923, Nadine spent her early life in a small town called Springs near Johannesburg. In those days, it was a mining and industrial town near the eastern tip of the 120-mile long gold-bearing ridge, the Witwatersrand.

It was here, when she first saw the unfairness in the way the African miners were treated, that her humanitarian feelings were awakened. She has developed these feelings throughout the more than 20 books she has written.

Nadine is the daughter of Jewish immigrants. Her father, a jeweler, was born in Russia and her mother was of British descent. At first Nadine was sent to a day school, a convent near her home. But her mother withdrew her from school when she was 11, saying the company of other children would aggravate her too-rapid heartbeat, which was considered a disability. She was also forbidden to do any strenuous activity, including ballet dancing which she enjoyed passionately.

It was at this stage that the young Nadine turned to books and writing as comfort and companionship for the long, intense loneliness she was to experience because of the very limited contact she had with other children.

Nadine's main achievement has been to move the South African novel into a new sphere. She is one of the founders of a new tradition in literary expression which shows the southern African reality in its own terms, and not in reference to Europe. This type of movement has taken place in a number of countries that have freed themselves and their cultures from colonial rule since the middle of this century.

Later she found that her heart complaint may not have been a problem, but rather an unconscious effort by her domineering mother to protect her. Perhaps, however, it was these solitary years that made Nadine into the world-class novelist she has become. She has said of her growth into adulthood that when the "invincible summer" of her teenage years ended, so there grew in her a loathing for racism.

Nadine studied at the University of the Witwatersrand in Johannesburg and in 1946 married Gerald Gavronsky, but the marriage ended after three years. In 1952 she married Reinhold Cassirer. They live in a suburb of Johannesburg.

World acclaim This great novelist began by writing short stories and plays. The first adult story she ever had published, "Come Again Tomorrow," appeared in a South African journal of current affairs, *Forum*, in 1939. Her first play was published in 1949, and her first collection of short stories, *Face to Face*, was published in South Africa in 1949 and re-published overseas in 1953 under the new title of *The Soft Voice of the Serpent*. This collection showed her deep sensitivity to the smallest details of life. It made an immediate impact and set her on the road as a writer of fiction. Her first novel, *The Lying Days*, published in 1953, revealed an inborn talent that she was to develop to world acclaim.

In 1971 she wrote *Guest of Honour* in which she tried to describe the wider African problem. It brilliantly evokes the beauty of the rural area near Johannesburg where the story unfolds around characters from different racial groups. Because of her outspoken views on the political situation in South Africa and on matters of sex, some of her books were banned for periods of time in her home country. The novel, *Burger's Daughter*, was banned by the government at the same time as it won a coveted local literary prize.

Interpreting reality More than most other South African authors, Nadine's work has recorded in fiction the havoc apartheid has caused on private lives. She writes mainly about racism, the crisis of liberal values, the nature of historical consciousness and sexual politics, approaching her subjects with compassion and humanity. A passionate interpreter of the South African reality, Nadine has based much of her imaginative work on happenings in the country. Her work is often seen as a fictional description of South Africa from 1953 until the present.

Although Nadine is considered by many literary critics as one of the finest living English language novelists, she has written and published almost as many volumes of short stories that are also very highly acclaimed. She has 10 novels and eight collections of

short stories to her name.

She also writes essays and literary criticisms, and is a frequent contributor to international literary reviews. She writes for television and is involved in literary workshops, especially for the Congress of South African Writers and the African National Congress's cultural wing. She has said that she hopes to use some of the financial reward from the Nobel Prize for Literature to help build a post-apartheid culture in South Africa, by stimulating indigenous literature—not only in English, but in all the local languages as well.

Nadine Gordimer. As a child she aspired to be a ballet dancer. But circumstances in her childhood led to her becoming a writer.

The second birth Coming from a traditionally European-oriented background, Nadine came into contact with a large circle of black writers, critics and artists in the '50s. She has said, "People like myself have two births, the second one is when you break out of the color bar."

Throughout the '70s she became more politically outspoken and now describes herself as a socialist in her general outlook. She has always lived in South Africa, remaining steadfast to her political, social and literary beliefs through difficult times, during which many other writers went into exile. Although an outspoken critic of apartheid in her private capacity, she has constantly disclaimed any political affiliation, wanting her work to be judged only from a literary perspective.

Nadine is no stranger to literary awards. She has received a number of local and international awards in recognition of her powers as a writer of fiction. She has won three CNA awards, one of South Africa's most sought-after literary honors. She won the coveted British Booker Prize in 1974 for her novel *The Conservationist*.

Winning the Nobel Prize for Literature was the culmination of Nadine's long history as a successful, but also an idealistic and socially concerned writer—a great honor to one of the world's greatest writers.

Albertina Sisulu

Veteran black leader Nontsikelelo ("non-SI-KI-lay-lo") Albertina Sisulu, one of South Africa's most outstanding and morally courageous women, has played a major role in the liberation movement for over four decades. The hardships of raising a large family while her husband, Walter Sisulu, was imprisoned for life have never deterred her from her belief in the fight for justice and equality and her commitment to women's rights.

Supportive from the start As the second oldest in a large rural family, when her mother died Albertina had to give up school for two years to nurse her baby sister. She was only 15 years old at the time. Luckily her grandparents were able to help her complete her high school education. But she had to become a nurse as it was a shorter training course than her preferred profession of teaching. She had to take care of and support her four younger siblings financially at this time. This supportive woman has never had a normal family life, neither as a child nor as a mother.

Because of the family's involvement in the anti-apartheid struggle, her husband has spent most of their married life in jail, Albertina has herself been jailed and banned, and her children have been jailed and in exile at times. There were times when she did not even know her children's whereabouts—a very painful experience for a mother. Her husband, Walter, was released from jail in 1989.

Albertina said that as a child growing up she was not disturbed by the political situation as their grandfather had "cattle and sheep, and fields to plow." However, once she was nursing in a Johannesburg hospital, she began to see the unfairness of discrimination against black people. She accompanied her fiance, Walter Sisulu, to many political meetings, often being the only woman to attend. By the time they married in 1944, she was well acquainted with the liberation movement and very inspired by the speeches she had heard.

Concern for women's issues Her concern for women's issues began at this early stage when she joined the ANC Women's League in an attempt to improve the lot of women, often the ones who suffered the most as they tried at the same time to earn a living and raise their families. Realizing not all women wanted to join the ANC, but needed a more universal and perhaps less political women's movement, Albertina and other women's leaders formed the Federation of South African Women (FEDSAW) in the mid-1950s. It attracted women trade unionists, churchwomen and others concerned with the hardships women had to endure. In 1983 Albertina became the third president of this organization which coordinated various groups working on women's rights and education.

Under FEDSAW women worked together to resist the attempt by the government to make them carry identity documents like the men did. The defiance campaign led to 20,000 women marching on the government buildings to hand in a petition. Albertina was at the forefront of this march and from then onward the government harassed her for her political beliefs and activities.

At the funeral of a fellow political activist. Albertina dedicates her life to the struggle against apartheid and an unjust society.

Other members of Albertina's family

The Sisulu name has for many decades been intertwined with the liberation struggle in South Africa. Walter Max Ulyate ("ul-YAH-tee") Sisulu, Albertina Sisulu's husband since 1944, was imprisoned for life with Nelson Mandela and a number of other African National Congress (ANC) members for planning acts of political sabotage and revolution. Born of a poor family, he had to leave school when he was 15 years old to earn a living and help support his family. In 1940 he joined the ANC and worked his way up to a senior position, running the organization in the Transvaal province. At the end of that decade he was voted Secretary-General. He worked tirelessly for the organization until his final imprisonment. He was one of the first ANC members to be released from life imprisonment in 1989, some months ahead of Nelson Mandela.

Son Zwelakhe ("zway-LAAH-ki") Sisulu, one of five children, became a journalist after completing his high school education. He was responsible for forming the Media Workers' Association of South Africa. He has been jailed, banned and placed under house arrest for his work as an activist. In 1984 he was awarded a Niemann Fellowship to study at Harvard University in the United States. He was then made editor of the *New Nation*, a newspaper, in 1986, but was again arrested, and released only after 950 days in detention. He is married and has two children.

One of his brother's, Max Sisulu, is an economist for the ANC. Both Max and his sister, Lindiwe ("lin-DEE-way"), spent a number of years in exile, and Jogomsi, an adopted son, also spent a number of years in jail for his political activity.

Persecution It was shortly after the march in 1958 that Albertina was first jailed with a number of her peers. She was again detained in 1963 for three months in solitary confinement, and then released without being charged. She was one of the first women to be treated in this way and says it was one of the worst experiences of her life as jail conditions were disgraceful. Trying to force her to talk about ANC activities, interrogators told her untruths about her children.

From 1964, for over 16 years, she was served with a number of banning orders. For 10 years she was placed under house arrest: she could not receive visitors and had to be in her home from 6 p.m. to 6 a.m. every day. She was not allowed near any educational institution or court of law. It was very complicated for Albertina, living in Soweto, Johannesburg, to get permission to visit her husband who was in jail over a thousand miles away on Robben Island off Cape Town. Through all this Albertina continued to work, only retiring in 1982 after 42 years in the nursing profession.

Leader of her people In 1983 a major nationwide umbrella organization, the

United Democratic Front, was formed to unite the people and the movements that resisted the apartheid government—and to give them direction.

By now publicly acclaimed as the Mother of the Nation, Albertina, although in detention again, was elected co-president. As a veteran political leader, she feels her election to this position, right at the top of an organization dominated by men, was because of her long and unwavering track record. She was at the front of the anti-pass demonstrations, and she was among the women who closed the schools and set up alternative classes when segregated education was introduced by the government. And Albertina led the women who stopped the men wasting their meager salaries drinking in government-sponsored beer halls during the Soweto uprisings in the '70s.

Although circumstances prevented Albertina from becoming a qualified educationist herself, she still believes very strongly that with education people are equipped for life. "You can go anywhere and express yourself, you can uplift your people by teaching them to find what is right for themselves."

Belief in non-violence Throughout her life Albertina has been a strong advocate of non-violence and believes that the only way forward is to establish a non-racial South Africa. She says of her multi-racial but divided country, "The feeling is we are all here to stay, so everyone must be involved in working for the future South Africa we want."

At one time Albertina Sisulu and one of her sons, Zwelakhe, who was living with her, were banned at the same time. The law stated that banned people were not allowed to speak to each other. Said Albertina to one of her friends, "What was I supposed to do? Not ask him what he wanted for breakfast?"

Albertina receiving a present from her husband Walter Sisulu on her birthday, celebrated with the Archbishop Desmond Tutu and other ANC members who were released from jail at about the same time as Walter.

Helen Suzman, a gutsy woman who fought against racial discrimination on every front, and helped bring world attention to the plight of those who did not have the vote in South Africa.

Helen Suzman

Helen Suzman, a remarkable woman and a courageous South African, retired from politics only a few years ago after 36 unbroken years in opposition to the government. For 13 years she was the lone voice in a hostile world where she was at times outnumbered in Parliament by more than 100 to one. It takes great determination to stand up to the continuing flood of political venom—she was often taunted with abuse, jibes, insults and mass uproar. But she never flinched in her fight for the right of each individual to be treated justly and fairly, regardless of background, status or community group.

Conscience of the nation A clever, articulate and tough woman, Helen represented the liberal conscience of the nation in the world of formal Parliamentary politics. In championing the cause of human rights, including women's issues, she constantly challenged the government on its less than clean record on these matters.

Helen's concept of simple justice and fair play has been the source from which all else flows. In her long career she has fought to rid the country of discriminatory laws like those that allowed job reservation or forbade relationships and marriage between different racial groups, or the laws that stopped black people living and working wherever they chose. She fought for the right for workers to form trade unions freely and to use their power to improve their lot in life. She fought the forced removal of people, the unequal education and welfare systems, the repressive functions of the police and the prisons.

Her deep commitment to liberal values drove her to visit prisoners, address the government on behalf of political detainees, defend the freedom of the press, stand up for the rights of the oppressed, speak out for civil liberties, and argue in favor of giving the vote to all South Africans. She brought to the nation and the world's attention political assassinations, sought a stop to capital punishment, intervened when electricity was cut off to poor black townships in mid-winter due to political unrest. She has also expressed her outrage at the violence committed in the townships.

The list is endless, the thanks and praise from the hundreds of people she has helped both individually and as groups is boundless. On her retirement Nelson Mandela wrote to her from his prison cell saying, "...the consistency with which you have defended the basic values of freedom and the rule of law over the last three decades has earned you the admiration of many South Africans..."

Concern for humanity Helen was most concerned with what apartheid would do to people in this society and to the future generations. She was very impatient with those who pushed aside decent human values, very angry with those who enforced injustice. She has proudly said, "The minutes [in Parliament] record my vote against every bit of repressive legislation this country ever introduced."

Through her actions in Parliament she showed South Africans the yardstick for measuring what "is" against what "should be," for what was happening against what should and could have been put in place politically. She asked a lot of probing questions in Parliament.

When the answer seemed to hide the truth, she demanded more information, exposing many irregularities in this way.

Interest in women's issues Helen has constantly challenged the prejudices against women in public life and felt it her duty to take a personal interest in women's issues in Parliament. Although the major force motivating her life is the broad issue of discrimination, she says, "I am a feminist. My feelings on racial issues have to do with injustice; and many injustices are meted out to women." She has fought stoically to put these injustices right, championing for old laws to be changed and new ones introduced, such as laws that will give all women equality with men, equality in the workplace, the right to an abortion or a fair deal in divorce.

Over the years not many more than two dozen women have been voted into Parliament in South Africa, but the contribution made by many of those who have braved this very male-dominated arena is undeniable. Women have stood for a broad spectrum of political parties from the most liberal through the middle-of-the-road groups to the Nationalist Party, which was responsible for apartheid legislation. But almost all of them have been concerned with issues immediately affecting their communities, and especially women.

Worldwide respect As one of South Africa's most widely respected politicians—both at home and in the international arena—Helen has been honored in many ways. Shortly after she retired in 1989, she was made a Dame of the British Empire by Queen Elizabeth II in recognition of her tireless fight for human rights and a just society. A decade earlier she shared the United Nations Award of the International League for Human Rights with the late Martin Luther King, and has twice been nominated for the Nobel Peace Prize.

She was often asked the question, "Why do you go on?" especially during the 13 long, lonely years she was the only member of her party in Parliament. Her reply: "This is the question I asked myself every day—why go on? You keep on because while you are living here you can't do nothing about it. Really, you can't, unless you're the type who can put on blinkers and go play golf or lie beside the pool or just shop all day long."

Apart from her impact on the lives of many individuals, she made a contribution of monumental proportion to the country. At a critical point in South African political history, she kept alive a belief in the liberal values of human dignity, individual freedom, and the rule of law. She demonstrated the value of the Parliamentary system of government, and set a standard of excellence in opposition which will stand as a model for generations to come.

Her role in contemporary political history of keeping alive basic human values has been inspirational not only for the current generation, but will remain important long after the era of apartheid has faded.

Of her long and distinguished career, she says modestly, "It is hard to say that one has achieved anything except, I think, to keep certain values alive in this country—certain democratic values." There are millions of South Africans who will thank her simply for this.

A hostel where miners live, away from their families. Helen Suzman condemned the migrant labor system because it tore families apart.

Mamphela Ramphele

Dr. Mamphela Ramphele ("MUM-pay-lah RUM-fay-lay"), Vice-Chancellor of the University of Cape Town, is probably the most senior woman in South Africa's academic world. Her brief is to ensure one of South Africa's biggest and best universities lives up to its new-found principle of being non-racist and non-sexist.

She is determined to use her appointment to give black students, and particularly women, a fair chance in what has been for many years in the past a traditionally liberal, white, male-dominated university. She will succeed just as she has succeeded in using her career to better the lot of people who are at a disadvantage, just as she has succeeded in the past in turning personal disaster into a triumph for a struggling community.

"Fatal attraction" Mamphela is no stranger to education as both her parents were teachers in the northern region of the country. Although her family was far from wealthy, she managed to study medicine, becoming one of the first black women in the country to complete this course. By the time she was 30 she had established a community health center and program in the eastern Cape. At university she met the famous black leader, Steve Biko. She calls her relationship with him "fatal attraction"

as she became politically aware and active. Mamphela, Steve's girlfriend until he died in detention in 1977, said her relationship with him had provided her with the inspiration to scale academic heights, and that his political ideals had forged the foundations of her work.

One day police arrived at her clinic with an order that banished her to a region in the north of the country many hundreds of miles away from Steve and her friends. She is convinced that she was banned because of her very close relationship with Steve, as on her own, she says, she was no threat at all.

Mamphela Ramphele. Her slightness belies the will of steel that has seen her through dark days and enabled her to work unceasingly for the good of her community in the face of adversity.

Dark days Mamphela was dumped in the middle of a very poor rural area where at first she did not even speak the language of the local people. The green hills, scarred by furrows of red soil erosion, were quite foreign to her. But this indomitable woman could see that she was badly needed in the community, even if they at first seemed hostile to her presence.

Her despair turned to grief when she heard of Steve's death, but the birth of his child, a boy she called Hlumelo ("shlu-MAY-lo"), which means new sprig off the old branch, raised her hopes. Those were the darkest days of Mamphela's life, but she now talks of the people who helped her and not of the pain of the time. Modestly, she says that at bad periods in her life there has always been someone to help her become a "whole person" again.

Giving to the community Mamphela was determined not to let the loneliness of banning overwhelm her. Instead she decided to channel her anger into positive action and get involved with the community. She found the 50,000 people of Lenyene area had no doctor, and working 12 hours a day and more, she turned an old shopping complex into a clinic. Soon word of her strength, warmth and love spread through the community. She built, staffed and ran a clinic with funds begged from the private sector and from overseas. She also established a day care center for over 100 children from destitute families. With boundless energy, Mamphela set up a literacy program which included a library and a scholarship fund, although over 60% of her community over the age of 25 were illiterate. She started community health care programs in which health workers go to the villages to give lectures on sanitation, hygiene and dental care. She organized a community vegetable garden, a sewing and knitting club and a brick-making cooperative run by women.

Realizing her knowledge of tropical medicine was limited, she applied to the state to ease her banning order and allow her to attend a year-long course so that she could look after her patients better in this humid region. She was refused, but undaunted, managed to qualify through a correspondence university.

With determination she turned her prison—she was banished to this area for six years—into her home. After her banning order was lifted, she stayed on in the community where she was so needed, even after she married one of Steve's friends who lived many hundreds of miles away, and with whom she had a second son. She only left the community she came to call home when a replacement doctor had been found.

Winning battles Mamphela, who also has a commerce degree, was appointed

Mamphela with
Ellen Khuzwayo,
a women's rights
activist.

a research fellow at the Cape Town university to help complete the Carnegie Inquiry into Poverty. She co-authored a book on poverty which achieved international recognition, and was appointed as a social anthropology lecturer at the university. Because of her work in the field of poverty, she was asked to join the Independent Development Trust (IDT), a board set up to alleviate poverty.

Mamphela says that, apart from her demanding role at the university, her worlds include her academic research, the IDT, her two sons and her home. It takes time to juggle all these spheres and time is what she lacks most, says Mamphela with feeling.

Mamphela does not belong to any political party, but is committed to a non-racial, non-sexist, democratic South Africa. She is particularly concerned about the education of black students and says her prime aim is to see the university become a truly African institution in the broadest sense. She says there should be a change of attitude toward higher education in her country by both white and black students as well as the teaching staff. She feels the sooner there is a fully integrated education system, the sooner the country will be able to educate children to realize their full abilities. She sees many battles ahead in her role at the university, but when she has decided to do something, she does not rest until it is done.

Erika Theron

Dr. Erika Theron was an Afrikaner, but an Afrikaner with a difference. By her own admission she was a formidable woman, but according to the many who stand in awe of her—academics, politicians, very important South Africans—her loyalty, civility and, above all else, her human compassion will set her down in history as one of the nation's most sophisticated rebels.

Lone woman rebel Erika is probably the only woman in a line of great Afrikaner rebels dedicated to their culture but against the apartheid government. She displayed her rebellious nature early in life. At junior school her classmates encouraged her to enter a no-go zone on the school veranda. When challenged by the school principal in English, which was not her native tongue, she stood her ground, saying in bad English, "I pays my moneys and I walks where I likes," meaning that she too had rights and was determined to exercise them.

Born in 1907, at the end of the Victorian era, Erika's feisty stance in life could seem surprising. But a clue to this remarkable woman's character lies in her childhood. She was of Scottish and Afrikaner descent and from a family of doers. The family moved to Tulbagh, a small town in the Cape province, before Erika was born. Her father soon became mayor of the town. As the youngest of seven children, she was always the center of attention which she felt gave her a competitive edge in any situation. It was her father who encouraged her to grow, or as she put it in an interview shortly before her death in 1990, "I was a spoilt little brat and he took me everywhere I wanted to go."

Erika entered the Afrikaans university of Stellenbosch, and completed a bachelor's and then a master's degree in economics. In the '30s she studied at Berlin university and witnessed the rise to power of Hitler and the Nazis.

On her return to South Africa, she began, as a social worker, what was to become her lifelong involvement and concern for the underprivileged in South Africa.

After completing her doctorate she was appointed professor of sociology, one of the first three women to be given this position at her university. At the same time, she became the first woman mayor of the university town.

After 36 years of active contribution to the university, she retired so as to be able to head a government commission that would change her life and her view of the ruling Nationalist government that she had supported.

Winning over a community The 20-member multi-racial commission, dubbed the Theron Commission, was to make an exhaustive investigation into all matters affecting the Colored community which had some years before been disenfranchised, that is, not allowed to vote, by the ruling Nationalist government.

At first the Colored community was skeptical about Erika, seeing her as a supporter of the Afrikaner government. But soon her obvious disgust at the damage the apartheid laws had done to the community, and her determination to set it right, won her their lasting admiration.

For three years Dr. Theron and her group traveled the country gathering information and then made their recommendations to Parliament. It is Erika's transformation during this period that led her to say to members of the Colored community, "I am ashamed of my people," an admission which makes her stand out above any other Afrikaner woman of her time.

Erika's strongest reaction was against the Group Areas Act—"the cruellest Act of all"—which forced people of different groups to live in separate areas and allowed the government to move people against their will from one area to another. Although still a supporter of the Nationalist Party at this stage, she felt she had to make her opposition to the Act quite clear. She addressed many meetings after the report was published, where she gave her well-researched reasons for her opposition. Her report also recommended the removal of the Mixed Marriages Act and the Immorality Act, all of which caused so much bitterness, hostility and distrust between the different people of South Africa.

The pillars of the separate development, or the apartheid policy, of the Nationalist government were:
- the Group Areas Act which forced people of different groups to live in separate areas and allowed the government to move people against their will from one area to another;
- the Mixed Marriages Act which forbade people of different race groups to intermarry;
- the Immorality Act which forbade sex between people of different race groups; and
- the Population Registration Act which classified people into different race groups at birth depending on their parent's race group.

Parliament House. Erika Theron died a disillusioned woman because she worked so hard for a mixed Parliament without success.

Defeat at eighty? At 80 years of age Erika admitted defeat. After slowly turning away from much of the Nationalist Party ideology over the decades, she decided in 1986 to resign from the party, rather than to continue her fight from within. She said at the time, "I was fed up with what was going on. I found enough reason to be disappointed, disillusioned, disenchanted. I had hoped that by now [10 years after the Theron Commission] we would have a mixed Parliament [Parliament made up of all the different races in the country]."

Not long after that, she resigned from the Afrikaner church. And then as a final statement of her beliefs in human rights, first expressed as a young schoolgirl, she rejected one of the government's top honors, the State President's Award. But as always Erika's rejection was discreet and polite. Instead, she said, one of her proudest memories was being called "an honorary Colored" by a Colored academic.

Strong, courageous, doughty Dr. Erika Theron will be remembered for her honesty and integrity. Most of all, she will be remembered for her courage to stand up to her entire people, and tell them they were wrong, that she rejected apartheid, and that they should too.

Fighting for their rights A woman of great courage, Erika fought for the carrying out of the report's recommendations long after the government had tried to ignored them. To make her point, she at one time turned to the English-language press, instead of her native-tongue Afrikaans newspapers, which she felt were government supporters and would not publish her story.

Because of their admiration for Dr. Theron, the university set up for the Colored community invited her to be their chancellor once her work on the commission was completed. She filled this post for more than 10 years until her retirement.

Miriam Zenzile Makeba

Mama Africa has returned home. After more than 30 years of star-studded exile, Miriam Zenzile ("ZEN-zee-lay") Makeba has again sung to her fans in her home country. She still has that sweet, clear voice that set Sophiatown, near Johannesburg, ablaze when she made her debut in the '50s and the same nightingale sounds that introduced the Western world to the "click songs" of the Xhosa language when she took the international world by storm almost four decades ago. Unlike many stars who have made it to the top, Miriam stands out as a modest woman with a quiet dignity and an intense pride in her people and in Africa.

Early influences The first musical influences on young Miriam were the school and church choirs and performances of Ella Fitzgerald and Billie Holiday on old gramophone records. Born in 1932 to a domestic worker turned medicine woman and spiritual healer, a *sangoma*, her first big break came when she joined a local band.

She was 20 years old then, and newly-divorced. The '50s was a time of intense creativity in South Africa, and Miriam was swept along with it. She took the lead in a jazz opera, *King Kong*, based on the life of a murdered black boxer. After that she left for France for the premiere of a film she had sung in, and which had

Miriam Makeba was finally allowed to return home in 1990 after more than 30 years in exile.

been made secretly in South Africa.

She was the first black South African singer to gain international fame and sang in Carnegie Hall in New York, Royal Albert Hall in London and Olympia Music Hall in Paris. Miriam married South African jazz exile Sonny Pillay—for three months. Later she met Harry Belafonte and followed him to New York. In America she sang on TV in front of 60 million people and performed in front of Duke Ellington and Miles Davis. She also sang to John F. Kennedy on his birthday, where she met Marilyn Monroe. But tragedies struck as quickly: Her only daughter died unexpectedly, and she had an almost fatal battle with cancer. She also survived an airplane crash.

> Miriam Makeba can sing in any number of diverse languages: Xhosa, Zulu, Swazi, Sotho, Shangaan, Spanish, Portuguese, Hebrew, Yiddish, Indonesian, and, of course, English.

Forbidden to return Under Harry Belafonte's guidance, Miriam consolidated her career and her success. Her attacks on the racial policies in her home country brought the wrath of the South African government on her, and they refused to allow her back into her country, not even for her mother's funeral. She appeared before the United Nations as a vocal anti-apartheid campaigner and highlighted the plight of her people in a number of her most popular songs, making millions around the world aware of the conditions of fellow black South Africans.

For two years she was married to an old friend, Hugh Masekela, whom she had known since she was just 14. He is now a world-famous jazz musician. They remain good friends and Miriam says Hugh can still write and arrange a song for her without even seeing her—"he knows me so well."

Late in the '60s she married an American militant activist, Stokely Carmichael, a member of the Black Panthers. A number of her concerts and contracts were cancelled as she was shunned because of her relationship with Stokely. They went to live in Guinea in Africa, but the marriage ended. Miriam remained in the country, combining her own recording and concert work with cultural and diplomatic missions for the Guinean president. Her voice, her beauty and her charm made her a favorite of many African presidents, and she sang at a number of independence celebrations across the continent.

More recently Miriam worked with Paul Simon on his very famous *Gracelands* album and concerts and defended it as a musical happening, criticizing the press for trying to turn it into a political issue. She also performed with Dizzy Gillespie on a two-month European tour and worked with Bill Cosby on a show.

Never forgot her roots While abroad Miriam was never swallowed by Western values. She never forgot her roots and says that she always found time to do her traditional rituals, no matter whether she was in Hollywood or Paris. It was because of this that she found the South African government's refusal to let her return home for her mother's funeral particularly hard to bear. One of her first pilgrimages once allowed back into her home country in 1990 was to her mother's graveside "to tell her I am back."

South Africa had stayed with Miriam all the years she lived abroad in exile "like an unhealed wound, but like all refugees I knew I would go home one day." That time has come. Today Miriam makes her home in South Africa, but as her career continues her work commitments take her all over the world much of the time. Her somewhat nomadic life which led to her setting up home in the United States, France, United Kingdom, Belgium, Guinea, Ghana and Senegal has ended.

Miriam on stage.

While Miriam was abroad, she often acted as surrogate mother to exiled South Africans, looking out for them whenever she moved to a new country or heard news that fellow countrymen were arriving. She would rush out to see if she could help them or offer them temporary accommodation. Miriam adds that South African musicians, especially ones in exile, helped her retain her identity by encouraging her to sing her own kind of music and to resist imitating famous Americans. She is one of the few singers who has retained a very high profile by singing songs almost entirely from and about her own culture.

Miriam admits she has a bad temper, but says flare-ups are all over in five minutes and she does not bear any grudges. This makes her very defensive about her five marriages and has enabled her to remain friendly with most of her ex-husbands, although she feels that once a marriage is over there is little point in trying to drag it on or revive it.

Miriam is very much her own woman and stresses her own dignity and independence when she says, "I have never been Mrs. Anybody, I am Ms. Makeba." When she entered into the relationship with Bagehot Bar, her current husband—she no longer lives with him, although they are not divorced—she let him know that if he wanted to be married to her, it was on her terms. He would come to live in her home while she was in Guinea, and could return to his family in African tradition while she was working abroad. Hers is an African wisdom liberated under an American style.

Miriam Makeba says of her life and her success, simply, "Singing makes me happy!"

chapter six

A Lifetime

T he roles women play at the different stages of their lives can be very varied because of the very different cultures that make up the South African society—the African tribal, Afrikaner, European-centered and Asian cultures, and a mixture of many of them. Also women's roles are dramatically different depending on whether they enjoy an urban life or live in the rural areas, whether they are members of the affluent middle class or the working class.

Birth

In rural African society the roles of men and women are very different and quite clearly defined. Childbirth is seen as being entirely the business of women: physically this means that men are rarely, if ever, allowed to be present at the birth, and ritually it means that anything associated with the birth is impure. Mother and baby must be careful not to do anything that will encourage evil spirits or magical attacks.

Thus the birth process takes place away from the rest of the society with only two or three midwives, usually older women, to assist the mother. The positions for giving birth vary from one tribe to another, but usually depend on what the mother prefers.

Opposite: A family in the homeland of Transkei. In rural African societies, men and women have very different and distinct roles.

Right: Women carry their children on their backs as they go about their work.

Difficult birth If a woman is having a difficult birth, there are a number of remedies. One tribe sometimes uses "sympathetic magic," which means that women in the vicinity loosen the clothes they are wearing to help her with the birth. By doing this, they all focus their positive will on her birth process and so help it to happen smoothly. In other cases a herbalist or priest-diviner may be called if labor is not going smoothly. Often the traditional medicines offered are very effective.

A traditional Zulu birth ritual was to give the new baby a medicine made from leopard's whiskers, salamander skins, lion's claws and, as the most important ingredient, when available, crushed meteorite! No doubt this concoction is rarely found today!

Special rituals Many African women perform special rituals as soon as the baby is born. In some tribes, the umbilical cord is cut immediately with a sharp piece of split grass. In others, the baby is immediately given special herbal medicines to drink and medicine is applied to its umbilical cord to dry it out. The mother's placenta is buried inside the hut and boiling water is poured over it in the belief that this will prevent afterbirth pains. Others bury the placenta and umbilical cord outside the hut in the *umsamo* ("um-SAA-mo"), or place of the spirits. Some babies are bathed immediately in cool water to remove the ritual heat associated with birth. In some tribes, a ritual fire is lit as soon as the baby is born and is not allowed to go out until the period of confinement has ended.

The mother and other closely associated women play an important role in the first feeding rituals, which are different for different groups. The baby's first mouthful for some is very fine millet porridge, for others it is cow's milk, while others have their first suckle on breast milk. In traditional societies, mothers breast-feed their babies for a long time, sometimes up to three years.

In traditional societies babies are breast-fed until they are about three years old.

Girl child, boy child When a baby is born, the midwife usually runs outside and shouts—twice for a girl, once for a boy. When a girl's birth is announced to her father in one tribe, water is sprinkled on his shoulder. (He would be tapped on the shoulder with a stick if it were a boy.) In another tribe two reeds are stuck into the grass roof of the hut to indicate the child is a girl and to remind male tribe members of the taboo to keep away from the hut. (Only one reed would be used to announce a boy's birth.)

Western values Although over a million African babies are born each year, the full tribal rituals are not often observed as many babies are born in urban areas and some of the rural babies may even be born in hospitals or clinics too. Many of the rural people have adopted Western values, and quite often modern birthing is a mixture of Western medical values and certain tribal rituals.

Urban babies are mainly born in hospitals in Western style with little or no ritual. In the more impoverished black urban communities, babies are often born at home with the help of a midwife.

Other communities In other urban and rural communities—English and Afrikaans, Colored and Asian—almost all mothers choose to have their babies delivered in hospital. In the past when it was not easy to get to hospitals from

Mother and child. Many birth rituals are no longer observed as people move into urban areas or adopt Western values, and babies are born in hospitals.

some of the far-flung rural areas, children were born at home with the help of a local midwife, and sometimes even a doctor who would travel to the farmstead if possible.

A special birth tradition exists among some of the more devout and traditional in the Malay community, part of the Colored group. Pilgrims returning from Mecca try to bring back with them a dried piece of the succulent plant that grows along the road to the holy shrine. This brown and withered stick is placed in a glass of water by the bedside of a mother as she is giving birth. In the water the stick expands and seems to bloom and is thought to be of psychological help to the woman in labor. Once the child is born the stick is dried again and put away till the next birth.

Childhood and school life

Traditional beliefs and roles In very traditional African society, a child has little formal schooling. Rather, he or she learns the skills and behavior from the older people. Girls used to learn their roles from older women, which meant that for many years they kept much of their tribal customs. But as the country began to industrialize and Africans moved to the urban areas, these ancient roles were no longer totally suited to the new lifestyle. Today almost all children have at least some years of Western education. But in rural areas girls have little chance of any significant education, and traditional beliefs and roles are strongly perpetuated.

From as young as six or seven years old, African girls in the rural areas learn to look after the babies in the family, carrying them around on their backs while their mothers are busy. Once they are physically strong enough, at about 10 or 11, girls start to help their mothers in the house and in the fields with agricultural work. Even the games the young girls play are about domestic matters like cooking, while dancing and music making are also an important part of their learning in a traditional society.

African girls in the townships Poverty means that in most households in the townships both parents are forced to work. There are also many homes headed by single women who have to care for the entire family, often on a small salary. Many an urban schoolgirl, already disadvantaged by the unfair education system for African youth, faces further disadvantage as she may have to take time off school to care for younger siblings while her mother is at work. Or she may have to leave school at an early age if there is not enough money for all the children to attend school.

In the past girls were usually made to leave rather than boys. But over the last decade or so, the number of African girls who graduate from high school has been increasing steadily. However,

Girls start to help out in the family at an early age, in the house or out in the fields.

African girls are expected to help a lot in the homes, learning to do the "women's work" of cooking, cleaning and housekeeping from an early age. Boys rarely do domestic chores.

Urban segregation White children growing up in an urban environment receive a fairly traditional and conservative upbringing. Both at home and at school, girls are often told that a woman is first a homemaker and mother. The family usually consists of mother, father and children, with the children being the central focus of family life.

Some children with working parents are sent to child care centers, while others have African nannies to take care of them at home. Even if mothers do not work, they usually employ a domestic worker who does the housework and often helps with child care too. Most affluent urban children go to nursery school for a year or two before they enter junior school at the age of six.

A non-racial school. More often than not white and non-white children go to segregated schools and have little contact with each other until later in life.

Indian children in their school uniforms.

The passage of school

Until recently all government schools were segregated, with white, Colored, Asian and African children going to separate schools. Attending school was enforced by law for all white, Colored and Asian children from the ages of 6 to 16. However, this law was not effectively enforced for the African communities.

Junior school, which has seven grades, is usually co-educational, that is both boys and girls attend the same school. There are five grades in high school, but it is not compulsory to complete them all. High schools are more often single-sex schools both for girls and boys, but there are also co-educational high schools.

Most schools are government run and funded, although there are private schools as well. Children are expected to wear a school uniform—girls wear dresses, or skirts and blouses, with a sweater or blazer if necessary. In the classroom girls and boys receive the same lessons, but on the sports fields they usually play different games.

In the white farming community most children attend boarding schools as distances are usually too great to travel to and from school each day. Some children, especially the younger ones, may go to boarding school during the week and join their families at home for weekends. Once they attend high school, they usually have to travel even farther to school, and only come home for school holidays.

School boycotts by urban African children

When the apartheid government came to power in the late '40s, it introduced racially separate schools with a different set of educational standards for African, Asian, Colored and white schoolchildren. In general the government hoped to train whites for professional and white collar jobs, while keeping a large semi-educated mass of African labor for manufacturing, the mines and other industries. Resentment of this policy of inferior educational standards built up over the decades, especially in the urban areas.

In 1976 a mass student movement decided on school boycotts as a show of disapproval for the system. Unfortunately the government met this action with a hail of bullets, killing a number of students. Resentment boiled over and within a short time student riots had spread to most urban black areas. The death toll ran to thousands as youths—both girls and boys—confronted police and the military in a campaign of defiance. Many school buildings were burned down in protest.

This situation was never totally resolved as the apartheid government, although improving the standard of black education a little, would not integrate the schools. It also refused to spend the same amount of money on education for black children as it did for white pupils. Black teachers were supportive of the students' demands as they too were aware of the inferior citizens such a system was creating. As a result many children rarely attended school for the next decade or more, and those who tried to were often faced with boycotts, student violence and a general lack of discipline. One of the first issues Nelson Mandela tackled when released from jail was to call on black youths to return to school. Schools are now being integrated and it is hoped that an improved education system will in some ways be able to help make up for many lost years.

A lone demonstrator. Some South African teenagers are more politically aware and concerned about injustices in their society.

Adolescence

In a Western-style society, a girl's teenage years are often filled with conflicts between the young person and the adults in her society as she tries to make the change from childhood to being accepted as an adult by the older generation. Most South African teenagers are no exception to this, as many say they cannot talk to their parents about things that really matter, especially about sensitive things like sex.

However, in the few traditional African societies that still practice puberty and initiation rites, young girls (and boys) learn a clear set of rules that help them make this transition. They are shown the behavior expected of one to another within their tribal structure. As more and more teenagers and young women leave the rural areas and head for the cities in search of work, they often have to learn, very quickly, how to deal with a new set of values and rules of behavior.

Because of South Africa's past political history, some teenage girls and boys are more politically aware and concerned about the injustices of the past and the way forward for a new future. High school children have set up groups to talk across the barriers of race and religious beliefs, and often discuss quite adult issues like rejecting racially segregated schools. Many teenagers are very serious about their role as the future adults and leaders in the country.

Rural rites and rituals In a traditional African society, puberty rites are usually carried out by young girls on their own or in small groups. The rituals are different from one group to the next, but generally the girls are secluded from society in a hut for the duration of their first menstrual period. In some societies the girls are given special herbal drinks or food, while in others each evening of the seclusion is marked by singing and festivities by the youngsters. Often, at the end of this seclusion, there is a sacrifice and a party to mark the girl's becoming a woman.

In some customs special initiation schools are held which girls attend for three to nine months. Discipline is tough and punishment is often in the form of harsh beatings. They learn the customs and rituals of their tribes and are taught about pregnancy, childbirth and motherhood. They also hear stories and parables of mythical figures and symbolic objects which teach them about fidelity, respect and the powers of priest-diviners and spiritual healers.

Once the young girls return home they are taken into society as women and are then expected to begin the search for a husband.

Initiation ceremony of the South Sotho people

Among some of the South Sotho people initiation schools are sometimes held for girls. About 10 girls attend the school at a time which begins with the new moon and lasts for a few months. First they are bathed in the river by their women teachers to wash away their girlhood. For the first few days at the school the girls are covered in black ash, but later they paint themselves with white clay. At this time they wear only a sheepskin apron, plaited grass ropes around their waist, a grass veil to cover their face and some white clay beads. Although the girls do not have to stay away from their kraal, their identity has to be kept a secret. At the school they learn the traditions and taboos of their tribe which they can in turn pass to young girls in later years.

Different views on sex

The different communities in South Africa have widely differing views on sex before marriage and premarital babies. The Afrikaners and the more conservative English-speaking communities are against premarital sex, and babies born out of wedlock are seen as bringing shame on the family. There are very few homes for unmarried mothers, but at the same time the law forbids abortions except under exceptional medical circumstances. The laws of inheritance also discriminate against children born out of wedlock, and biological fathers do not necessarily have to support their illegitimate children.

In the Indian community very few children are born out of wedlock. This is because the Indians have kept many of their traditional practices, which do not allow sex before marriage. In the Colored community premarital babies and their mothers are accepted with little discrimination, although premarital sex is not an accepted practice.

In the African societies, both urban and rural, there are few taboos concerning sex before marriage or premarital babies. The number of single-mother households is increasing all the time as rural women are deserted by their husbands who go to work in the cities or on the mines and often do not return to their homes. Urban women have sometimes said that the chauvinist attitude of many African men who expect their wives to feed, clothe and care for them along with the children is too stressful. They would prefer to make their way on their own with their children.

Urban girls South Africa's affluent, white, urban girls have much the same dreams and aspirations, needs and wants, problems and sorrows, as their peers in the Western world. They have perhaps a little less independence, as parents are generally more conservative about things like dating, drinking alcohol and using drugs, sex before marriage and the age at which they may leave home to live on their own.

Clothes and fashions are very important to teenage girls who, as in most parts of the world, want to act, look and behave like their peers, rarely wanting to stand out as individuals. Their social lives are made up of going to the movies, parties and discotheques, and the never-ending search for boyfriends. As many mothers do not work outside the home, they are often indulgent, driving their children to and from friends' homes, shopping malls and social occasions. (Public transportation is also very poor in South Africa.)

Although often taught traditional "women's" roles of being homemakers and mothers, these girls spend very little time helping in the home as many mothers employ domestic help. Because of their more sheltered and protected home life, girls are generally less mature than city girls in Europe or America. Once they have completed school—and quite a high number also complete some form of college or university education— many girls are set on finding a husband and setting up home.

However, not all girls follow this path. As more women climb the corporate, political and business ladders, so more role models are slowly developing for young girls. Marriage and motherhood is no longer the only or most important option, but rather just one of many paths teenage girls can tread.

The Afrikaners, and especially the rural families, tend to be more conservative, with the Christian religion playing an important role in family life.

Becoming mother Urban black girls would like to enjoy much the same life as their white counterparts, but economic constraints often prevent this. In many homes economic necessity forces both parents to work long hours, and teenage girls often have to take care of their younger brothers and sisters, help with domestic chores and at the same time get their homework and studies done. Less often now than in the past, girls would have to drop out of school either because there was not enough money for their education or so that they could go out to work at an early age to help support the rest of the family.

Black adolescents devote more of their time to politics at an early age, with girls taking part alongside boys in school boycotts, political demonstrations and the like. They are also more serious about their education and are keener about keeping track of serious developments in current affairs, avidly reading newspapers and watching TV.

Learning about make-up at a technical college. African teenage girls approach life more seriously than their white counterparts.

After high school, what then?

Today all children can have the opportunity of studying at any institution of higher learning after completing high school if their qualifications are suitable and they can afford the fees. (In the past race laws prevented this, with separate institutions for different racial groups.) However, disadvantaged backgrounds, economic constraints and the poor standard of education in the African community, and to a lesser extent the Colored and Asian communities, have made it difficult for young black women to enter a university or college. There is also still an attitude among many black communities that women "don't need" education, but this is changing. Because of these educational constraints, most of the four million or more black women who work do so in the manufacturing sector as skilled, semi-skilled or unskilled laborers, and are employed as domestic workers or as laborers on farms.

The adult literacy rate among the least privileged parts of the South African society is still very low and some women and men cannot read or write at all. This has led to a number of organizations running literacy classes, and quite often even grandmothers are seen hard at work by the light of a candle learning to read and write.

A high number of white women choose to be homemakers and mothers. Many black women cannot afford the luxury of this choice.

A university education Women have never been excluded from university education, but in the early years of the century it was rare for them to go to a university. Today a fairly high number of white women have the privilege of attending a university. Although not barred by law from any career, except certain underground mining jobs, women are still encouraged to work in the service industry. There is no clearly defined discrimination in the courses or careers women may follow at a university, but courses like engineering or physics have only in the last decade or so had a few women students. More women are taking up these professions, but the numbers are still very small compared to men. Because women have been able to enter some professions with less difficulty than others, there are much higher numbers of women studying for careers in law, psychology or school teaching for example. The para-medical field also attracts a large number of women, in physical therapy, radiography and, of course, nursing.

Unfortunately a large number of white women who complete university degrees or other qualifications, are doing it simply to fill in time before they get

Like women elsewhere, South African women are the backbone of the teaching profession.

married. Once married, they stop working, and very few ever return to their careers. However, this trend is changing as women become more career oriented, and want to realize their own ambitions instead of living through the achievements of their husbands, and for their children. This desire for self-fulfillment in work as well as a marriage and family is not yet common. But more and more women are seeing a career as a desirable option. Also more white women need to work to supplement their husband's income and help support the family.

Not many in the professions There are very few black women in the professions although they make up over 80% of the population. On top of the educational constraints and economic disadvantage, black women, with their white peers, face sexual discrimination in the workplace. As an added burden, there is still a lot of racial discrimination as well. However, teaching and nursing are seen as "women's work" by many, and women have become the backbone of these professions, although they do not often reach the very top as senior principals or school inspectors.

There is no compulsory military service for women. A few enter the forces voluntarily, but mainly in administrative positions as they are barred from active service.

Fun time at a disco. In the city, young people of different cultures and beliefs mix together more freely.

Courtship and marriage

The dating game is played out in so many different ways in South Africa. For some of the traditional rural tribes, courtship starts early, usually with the beginning of puberty. In the more conservative rural Afrikaner families, parents are often very strict with their daughters, not allowing them to date until they are in their late teens, and then it is usually with a large dose of adult supervision. City life is more cosmopolitan and has thrown different cultures and creeds together—Christian, Jewish, Moslem, Hindu, Greek, Italian, African, agnostic and many, many more—and families or couples have adopted rituals (or no rituals) to suit their cultures and lifestyles.

In some of the very traditional rural groups once young people are fairly committed to each other—this does not necessarily mean they will definitely be married—they may engage in a certain type of external love-making without penetration which is called intra-crural intercourse. Although the young people have the unwritten consent of their community for this form of love-making, certain missionaries have tried to condemn it.

The range of different wedding ceremonies is huge. It can be secular, where the couple is married in a registry office, signing a legally binding document in the presence of a magistrate and witnesses after verbally agreeing to the marriage. Or it can be religious, where the ceremony specific to the group or religion is carried out, as well as the signing of a document that is legally binding. Today many African women and men choose to have a Western marriage, but there are some rural people who still follow the traditional marriage procedures, with some still opting for arranged marriages.

The tribal way The tribal African idea of marriage is very different from the Western view. The importance of the group or tribe is utmost and individualism is not a valued concept. The continuity and growth of the group is very important, and people who do not marry and have children are seen as failing in their duty to the group. The final status of adulthood is reached when a person marries. In a tribal society marriage is seen not only as the link between woman and man, but even more importantly, as the link between two family groups and the moving of the woman from her family to her husband's family. The ongoing relationship between the living and the dead (the ancestors) of each family is also represented in the marriage.

In tribal societies there is also the possibility of woman-to-woman "marriage." A wealthy woman who has enough cattle to pay the *lobola*, may take a "wife" who will do all sorts of chores for her. It is quite normal for this wife to become pregnant by her "husband's" husband—which means her children may have to call a woman "father." This is of course a very rare occurrence, but explains how very different are the customs of certain tribes.

Marriage ceremonies are very different from one tribe to another and totally traditional marriages, which means arranged marriages, are not very common today. The bridegroom's father will approach the family of a girl they consider suitable and *lobola*, or bride-price, negotiations begin. There is a strict protocol for bride negotiations which can sometimes take a few years if the prospective husband is not wealthy enough to pay his bride-price quickly.

Lobola, or bride-price, is a very complex issue not easily understood by people not familiar with tribal ethics. This practice establishes a bond and mutual responsibilities between the two families. It involves the transfer of cattle from the prospective bridegroom to the bride's family. It is a guarantee of his economic status and is compensation to the bride's family for loss of her services.

A Zulu wedding. The bride, dressed in ceremonial clothes, is escorted to the home of her groom by members of her clan.

But most importantly, the *lobola* is proof of the seriousness of the man's intentions—cattle are very valuable both economically and traditionally in a tribal culture. It also helps to ensure that marital duties on both sides are carried out: If a man neglects or mistreats his wife, she can go back to her family and his *lobola* cattle would be forfeited. If she is unfaithful, she could be sent back to her family and the cattle returned, making her very unpopular in her parent's kraal, or home. Because of the importance of continuity in the tribal customs, a woman's ability to have a child is part of the *lobola* deal. If she is infertile, her family must provide a sister free or return the bride-price. Only if the bride-price is paid can the father claim the children as his own. Under the *lobola* system, a wife cannot be divorced unless she fails in her duties and she usually retains her own family name!

However, this system does not always adapt well to a Western lifestyle. Quite often in an urban environment, the bride-price is paid in cash and other consumer items which of course once spent offer little or no protection to the wife. From a modern perspective, bride-price can be seen as demeaning to women, with them being viewed as goods that can be bought. In a modern, urban society, the bride-price has lost its relevance, and for this reason many women feel that in modern marriages it should be eliminated.

The wedding feast Traditionally the payment of the last *lobola* beast means the preparations for tribal wedding celebrations can begin, but often the wedding takes place before all the bride-price has been paid. The bride and her parents collect presents for her in-laws. The wedding is a great feast lasting a number of days, where ritual ceremonies are enacted and there is much eating, drinking of traditional beer, dancing and singing. In a traditional environment, a woman's marriage is not seen as complete until she has had a child, especially a boy child.

Today not many marriages are carried out in the totally tribal way because the Western and Christian view of a marriage as the union of two individuals, rather than two families, is being adopted by the youth. Now that young men are able to earn their own living and are independent of their parents, they can pay their own bride-price and live where they choose, instead of with their parents. Most modern African couples now choose this route, which is viewed by their parents as socially unacceptable.

The traditional Malay wedding

Among the Colored people, the traditional Malay community still upholds many of the customs brought to South Africa some 300 years ago from Malaysia. When a man had decided on a woman of his choice he asked his father to ask her father for her hand in marriage. A few days before the wedding, the bride and bridesmaids, dressed in their wedding clothes, would call on friends personally to ask them to attend the wedding feast.

On the wedding day the bride wore a beautiful headdress and veil, and dressed in her first wedding dress, she welcomed her guests to the celebration. She did not go to the mosque for the ceremony, but was represented there by her father. She could then change into a second wedding dress before she rejoined her guests. If she was from a wealthy family she could wear as many as three or four dresses during the celebrations. Toward evening on the wedding day the bride was taken to her new home by her parents-in-law.

In traditional Moslem custom, a man may marry up to four wives, but this trend is not encouraged in South Africa.

What the West has taught Marriage is an undertaking most people are still taught to regard as both desirable and necessary. Often a single woman is looked on by others, as well as herself, as a failure. In African communities she can also be seen as a burden on her family. But things are changing, and as more career women are economically independent, they can make choices not open to the generations before them.

Western marriages are almost always preceded by an engagement. This is a legal undertaking to marry a person which can be upheld by law. It is usually effected by the man giving his bride-to-be an engagement ring. Before a traditional Western wedding takes place, women friends and family usually organize a tea party, or in more modern homes a drinks party, for the bride-to-be. Only women are invited and each brings a small gift for the new home she will set up after her wedding. Sometimes helpful advice about marriage is offered, but mostly this is now just a party to celebrate the last days of her "freedom."

The Christian wedding ritual is similar in all countries. Even when religion may not be that important, many South African women still prefer the glamor and ritual of a church wedding, with the bride wearing a long white gown, perhaps a veil, and with bridesmaids and flower girls in attendance. After the ceremony a celebratory reception or party is held, and then the married couple usually leaves for a honeymoon or holiday at some special destination.

Marriage and the law Marriages in South Africa are governed by a set of civil laws. However, certain groups of

Breaking with tradition

As society is undergoing rapid changes, there are some women who now do not want traditional weddings. Some young couples prefer to live together for a while, and if they do decide to marry, they often have a civil ceremony followed by a party or dinner, without any of the rituals of a traditional wedding.

With women's roles being very much in transition at the moment, and the roles of men and women within a marriage changing, there is an uncertainty about marriage. Frequently expectations are not met, and this has led to South Africa having one of the highest divorce rates in the world. Also, economic independence means women do not have to remain in a marriage for a meal ticket, but can afford to leave. However, life is not easy as a single woman or parent.

people such as Africans can choose whether to marry by Western custom, in which case the civil laws apply to them, or to marry by tribal custom, in which case the tribal laws prevail.

Recently the civil law has been amended to give women equal status with their husbands. In the past a husband had "marital power," which meant he could make all the decisions in the family and the wife could not disagree. In some cases a woman lost her status as an adult when she married and could not make any contractual agreements without the permission of her husband. He in turn could sell her property without her permission. This has been changed in recent times.

If Africans marry according to customary or tribal law, the status of the woman in the marriage is very different from that of a marriage under civil law. She is often unable to own property, and is usually subjugated to her husband, which means she has to obey him.

Although most westernized women in South Africa choose to take their husband's last name when they marry, it is legal for a woman to keep her own name. This practice is not yet common but is increasing in popularity, especially among professional and career women. In African society it is tradition for a woman to keep her own name.

A Western-style wedding for urbanized Africans— complete with white gown and veil for the bride and a three-piece suit for the groom.

Married life and the home

As the wedding ritual is so different from one culture to the next, so is the role of the new wife and the way she is expected to set up her new home. Some rural African families still maintain the traditional structure of the extended families, while others have changed some aspects as a result of westernization. Traditionally, a new bride would leave her parents' home to live with her husband's family, but today many young couples set up home on their own. This is mainly because the young man, who often has a job, has been able to pay the *lobola*, or brideprice, himself, rather than have his father pay it for him.

Polygamy, that is having more than one wife, is acceptable in most tribal African societies, but it is becoming less common. In a polygamous household the husband is the central figure. Each wife with her children, her possessions, the fields she works and her hut forms a sub-unit within the home. Under traditional law, the husband is responsible for his wife in much the same way as he is for his children. She is not really the owner of the property she tills, but is given the use of it by her husband. She also has the burden of collecting firewood, fetching water because there is seldom water piped to the homes, doing all the agricultural work and all the cooking, cleaning and caring for the

Polygamy

The issue of polygamy, or men marrying more than one wife, has led to a lot of discussion in recent times. In African tribal custom, men were, and still are, allowed to take more than one wife. However, most men had only one wife unless they were rich and could afford more. The tribal chiefs often had more than one wife. One of the reasons given for polygamy in historical times was that men were often engaged in war and there was a chance there were fewer men than women in society. In the traditional cultures, the individual was less important than the group. In the 20th century, this is not really the case, and the problems of polygamy, like jealousy, arise more often.

Today it is felt by many, especially women, that polygamy has outlived its time. They feel polygamy has lowered the respect for women, whereas in a monogamous marriage, a marriage with only one wife, women are more able to command equal respect with men. Women feel polygamy partly explains the lower social standing of women. As a counter argument some people say they prefer an open form of polygamy rather than a pretend monogamy with prostitution, promiscuity and infidelity added to it.

children. Although her subservience to her husband may seem to belittle the woman, her role in the society is very important in keeping the traditions alive.

Cramped quarters Although almost all newly married couples in the townships would like to set up their own home, there is such a severe housing shortage in these urban communities that many young couples are forced to live with their families for long periods. Sometimes, it is many years before they can hope to get a home of their own.

Most houses in these areas are very small, sometimes having only two or three rooms, and the newly married couple is forced to share with many members of the extended family. This lack of privacy and the conflicts of such confined living put a lot of strain on a new marriage. Even married couples from the more privileged groups find it quite difficult to afford to buy a home of their own, but usually they are able to find rented accommodation until they can save enough money to buy their own home.

Adjusting to a whole new way of life as a newly-married couple can be very trying in cramped quarters like this.

Young mothers. In the white urban community traditions and rituals of birth are all but lost.

Motherhood

In some cultures a marriage is not considered complete until the arrival of the first baby, while some women delay having children until they have established a career. They also tend to limit the size of their family to one or two children, while some actively decide not to have children at all.

Before a baby is born The pending arrival of a new baby is a special time for most mothers with some preferring not to work, but to prepare for the child's arrival. Others, by choice or necessity, work until the birth. In traditional African societies, it is believed the ancestors help in the production and nurturing of the unborn child and in this way the family heritage is continued. A pregnant woman becomes a valued member of the society as she is carrying a child that could perhaps become a great person and perpetuate the tribe or family group.

There are a number of tribal beliefs and taboos concerning both the mother and the unborn baby. Some say the sex of a child can be told according to dreams the mother has. If she dreams of crossing a full river or of a puff-adder, a type of poisonous snake, it means she is carrying a girl baby, while dreaming of a buffalo or a black and green snake means she is to have a boy. Some groups believe that they can change the sex of child by taking a medicine made from a specific lily root—if the root looks like a female genital the baby will become a girl, if the root looks like a male genital the medicine will make a boy baby. There are also a number of food taboos for pregnant women: Some pregnant women may not eat guinea fowl, a chicken-like wild bird, because the child will have a bird-shaped head. For some tribes, standing and eating when pregnant may cause the child to be born feet first, which is dangerous to the child at birth. Some women do not eat hot food because it is believed it will scald the unborn child, and eating a whole range of vegetables is taboo in some clans. Other superstitions include the mother not cutting her hair as it is seen as the breath or life force for the baby, or not wandering on certain paths in the bush that may abound with magic and witchcraft to harm her and the child.

The stork party In the white urban societies the rituals and traditions have in most part been lost many hundreds of years ago, as in most Western societies, but some little ritual is held before the birth. A number of women friends and relatives of the mother-to-be organize a party called a "baby shower" or "stork party," where they give the mother small gifts for the child and offer her advice on birth and child care. Men are excluded.

The more affluent and well-educated modern women attend pre-natal classes, that is classes preparing them for childbirth and child care. They also have access to the many books on these subjects. Slowly, fathers are being encouraged to take part in the mother's pregnancy and childbirth, but it is still a rare occasion for a South African father.

Where is the child care?

More privileged women can choose whether they want a career, a job and/or a family. But because most businesses and the government are male-dominated, there is very little infrastructure to help mothers juggle their career, their children and their home. Some of the more progressive organizations are beginning to offer day care for their employees' children. A number of the trade unions are also beginning to negotiate for child care facilities for working mothers.

The majority of black women work because the family would starve if they did not. But the burden of a poor urban woman's lifestyle as a working mother is enormous. As yet there is very little child care available, and only about one in every 600 children in the townships is able to find a place in a day care center. The rest have to be left with elderly baby-sitters or in the care of older sisters. The working mother has to sustain the entire household, sometimes with the help of her older daughters. Men rarely, if ever, help with the housework and cooking, and more and more frequently are seen as more of a hindrance than a help in the home.

Many African women live and work in the cities, but in the past were forced by law to send their children to their relatives in the rural areas. Today the laws have been scrapped, but many women still choose to do this because of the inadequate child care in the cities, and also for fear their children may become caught up in the urban evils of crime or drugs. In African custom, at least some of the hardships endured by mothers are compensated for by the fact that love and respect of mothers is held up to young men as one of the highest virtues.

Old age

While many Western women feel their useful lives are ending with the onset of old age, and some try to cling to the trappings of youth, for many traditional African women their twilight years bring status and the respect of their society.

In her earlier years a tribal woman has to be carefully aware of the ritual impurities that are determined by her body's cycles. Once a woman is older, all this falls away and she may behave with much more freedom. She may even be allowed to air her views in the council where men sit to discuss the local politics of the day and other important issues.

Life is leisurely for the white woman in her silver years as children have grown up and flown the coop.

The rural grandmother An aging rural African woman is seen to have filled her role in society as wife and mother as the number of her descendants—her grandchildren and later great-grandchildren—increases, and within the rural society this gives her great status. She is free to enjoy her relationships with her grandchildren, and is very important in teaching the children the ways of their culture as well as the ways of life. In the Bushman culture, for example, it is the grandmother who teaches the children to speak. A grandmother's age and status also means she no longer has to work hard in the fields and in the home, as her daughters-in-law take on this strenuous work and leave her to take care of the grandchildren.

African tradition gives much more importance to the extended family than do Western families in South Africa, and this adds to the grandmothers' role. Because there are so few child care facilities in the urban areas, many working mothers, worried about the effects of the city evils on their children, send them home to the rural homestead to be cared for by their grandmothers.

Even in urban society, black grandmothers play a major role in taking care of the children while their mother is at work.

State pensions are very small, barely enough to live off. In the past these pensions differed in the amount paid out depending on the race of the person, with whites being paid the most and Africans the least. In recent years an attempt has been made to even this out, but there is still very little state assistance for the elderly. Employers are encouraged to set up private pension plans for their staff but this does not always take place, especially among the lower income employees who are more often women. Retirement age for women is 60 years old while for men it is 65.

Unfortunately, because of urbanization and westernization, both the cultural heritage and the extended family system are breaking down. Where this happens, the life of an older woman is certainly no pleasure as she may find she has no place within her family. Also there are very few state old age homes, and state old age pensions are barely sufficient to live on.

Finding their own world In the more affluent families, especially among white South Africans, grandmothers have a more limited role because many mothers have house-help and nannies, and the norm is for a nuclear family. In a few homes, additional suites are built so grandmothers can live with the family. But often, grandmothers (and grand-fathers) live on their own in apartments, or move into retirement homes where they have the company and support of people their own age. But both these options mean they have little contact with their families, and especially their grandchildren.

A woman's life

The life of a South African woman, no matter her culture or her status, is full and complex. She is often the nucleus for her family, providing love, care and attention, making a home the best she can. Today many a woman is also climbing a career ladder, juggling her life to suit herself as well as many others. It is no easy road, but South Africa's women are known for their perseverance. They will reach the goals they choose.

Women Firsts

Sirimavo Bandaranaike

(b. 1916) She became the first woman prime minister in the world when her party, the Sri Lanka Freedom Party, won the general election in July 1960. Her husband was prime minister of Sri Lanka when he was assassinated in 1959. She led her husband's party to victory in the 1960 elections.

Sarah Breedlove

(1867–1919) Also known as Madame C.J. Walker, she was the first self-made millionairess. An uneducated African-American orphan from Louisiana, U.S.A., she founded her fortune on a hair straightener.

Nadia Comaneci

(b. 1961) The Rumanian girl was the first gymnast ever to achieve a perfect score (10.00) in the Olympic Games in Montreal in 1976. In all, she had 7 perfect scores at the Games.

Marie Curie

(1867–1934) A Polish-born French physicist, she is famous for her work on radioactivity. She was the first woman to win the Nobel Prize for Physics in 1903, together with Antoine Henri Becquerel. She was also the first woman to win the Nobel Prize for Chemistry in 1911.

Katherine Dunham

(b. 1910) American dancer, choreographer and anthropologist who was the first person to organize a black dance troupe of concert calibre, in 1940. A popular entertainer who toured the United States and Europe, she was also a serious artist intent on tracing the roots of black culture.

Amelia Earhart

(1897–?) She was one of the world's most celebrated aviators and the first woman to fly alone over the Atlantic Ocean on May 20–21, 1932. In 1935, she made a solo flight from California to Hawaii, the first person to fly this route successfully. In 1937, she set out to fly around the world with a navigator. Two-thirds through the distance, her plane disappeared in the central Pacific.

Gertrude Ederle

(b. 1906) One of the best known American sports persons of the 1920s, she was the first woman to swim the English Channel, on August 6, 1926. She swam the 35 miles from Cap Gris-Nez, France, to Dover, England, in 14 hours 31 minutes, breaking the existing men's record by 1 hour 59 minutes.

Dame Naomi James

The New Zealander is the first woman to sail round the world solo, in the cutter *Express Crusader*. She sailed from Dartmouth, England, on September 9, 1977 and reached the same port on June 8, 1978. It took her 265 sailing days to complete the journey.

Selma Lagerlöf

(1858–1940) The first woman and also the first Swedish writer to win the Nobel Prize for Literature in 1909. A novelist whose work is rooted in legend and saga, she is said to rank among the most naturally gifted of modern storytellers.

Lucretia Mott and Elizabeth Cady Stanton	They founded the organized women's rights movment in the United States. In 1948 they organized the first Women's Rights Convention in the United States. Mott (1793–1880) also actively campaigned against slavery, and worked for voting rights and educational opportunities for freedmen after the Civil War. Stanton (1815–1902) went on to work with Susan B. Anthony for woman suffrage.
Florence Nightingale	(1820–1910) An English nurse, she was the founder of trained nursing as a profession for women. Because of the comfort and care she gave to wounded soldiers of the Crimean War (1854–) during the night rounds, she was dubbed "The Lady with the Lamp." In 1860 she established the Nightingale School for Nurses, the first of its kind in the world.
Margaret Sanger	(1883–1966) She is the founder of the birth control movement in the United States and international leader in the field. In 1916 she opened the first birth control clinic in the United States. In 1927 she organized the first World Population Conference in Geneva, Switzerland. She was the first president of the International Planned Parenthood Federation.
Junko Tabei	(b. 1939) A Japanese housewife, she was the first woman to reach the summit of Mt. Everest on May 16, 1975. She was part of the first all-woman (and all-Japanese) team to reach the summit.
Valentina V. Tereshkova	(b. 1937) A Russian cosmonaut, she was the first woman to travel in space from June 16 to 19, 1963. She was in space for 70 hours and 50 minutes. She volunteered for the cosmonaut program in 1961, and was accepted on the basis that she was an accomplished amateur parachutist, although she had no pilot training.
Baroness Bertha von Suttner	(1843–1914) An Austrian novelist and pacifist, she was the first woman to win the Nobel Prize for Peace in 1905. In 1841 she founded an Austrian pacifist organization, and from 1892 to 1899 she edited the international pacifist journal *Die Waffen nieder! (Lay Down Your Arms!)*.
Mary Wollstonecraft	(1759–1797) An English writer and advocate of educational and social equality for women, she was the author of *A Vindication of the Rights of Women* in 1792, the first major piece of feminist writing. The book, on a woman's place in society, pleads for the illumination of woman's mind.

Glossary

African people	People descended from the original tribal groups in South Africa.
Afrikaner	A white person of Dutch descent, from about 1908 onward. Afrikaners were called Boers until this time.
Asian people	The large immigrant population from India as well as people from the rest of Asia and the East.
banning order	An order by the government restricting a person from a number of activities including political involvement, addressing meetings, being quoted in the media and the like.
black people	Include all Africans, Colored and Asians in South Africa.
Boer	A South African usually of early Dutch immigrant descent.
Colored people	People who originated from the inter-marrying of the very early Dutch and other European settlers with some of the African tribes as well as with the Malay women who were brought to South Africa by the Dutch when they first settled in the country some 300 years ago.
detention	The law allowed the state to hold people in jail, that is put them in detention, for long periods of time without bringing them to court for a trial.
homeland	An area set aside by the apartheid government for each different African tribal group to live in. The government forcefully resettled millions of people into these mostly rural areas.
impis	The body of African warriors; usually it refers to Zulu warriors.
kraal/s	A grouping of African rural huts to form the home of an extended family or even an entire tribe.
rondavel	A circular room or living space usually with thatched roof
township	The urban areas the black people are forced to live in on the outskirts of the white towns and cities under the apartheid system. Soweto is a township alongside Johannesburg.
veld	The open countryside.
white people	People of European descent.

Further Reading

Lawson, Don: *South Africa*, Franklin Watts, New York, 1986.
North, James: *Freedom Rising*, Macmillan, New York, 1985.
Paton, Jonathan: *The Land and People of South Africa*, Lippincott, New York, 1990.
Russell, Diana E.: *Lives of Courage: Women for a New South Africa*, Basic Books, New York, 1989.
Stengel, Richard: *January Sun: One Day, Three Lives, A South African Town*, Simon and Schuster, New York, 1990.

(Nadine Gordimer's books are *Burger's Daughter*, *The Conservationist*, *Guest of Honour*, *July's People*, *Jum and Other Stories*, *Late Bourgeois World*, *Lying Days*, *Selected Stories*, *My Son's Story*, *Six Feet of the Country*, *Soldier's Embrace*, *Occasions for Loving*, *Something Out There*, *Sport of Nature* and *World of Strangers*.)

Picture Credits

Index